Cambridge Elements

Elements in the Philosophy of Georg Wilhelm Friedrich Hegel
edited by
Sebastian Stein
Heidelberg University
Joshua Wretzel
Pennsylvania State University

HEGEL AND SPINOZA

James Kreines
Claremont McKenna College

Shaftesbury Road, Cambridge CB2 8EA, United Kingdom

One Liberty Plaza, 20th Floor, New York, NY 10006, USA

477 Williamstown Road, Port Melbourne, VIC 3207, Australia

314–321, 3rd Floor, Plot 3, Splendor Forum, Jasola District Centre, New Delhi – 110025, India

103 Penang Road, #05–06/07, Visioncrest Commercial, Singapore 238467

Cambridge University Press is part of Cambridge University Press & Assessment, a department of the University of Cambridge.

We share the University's mission to contribute to society through the pursuit of education, learning and research at the highest international levels of excellence.

www.cambridge.org
Information on this title: www.cambridge.org/9781009593243

DOI: 10.1017/9781009593205

© James Kreines 2026

This publication is in copyright. Subject to statutory exception and to the provisions of relevant collective licensing agreements, no reproduction of any part may take place without the written permission of Cambridge University Press & Assessment.

When citing this work, please include a reference to the DOI 10.1017/9781009593205

First published 2026

A catalogue record for this publication is available from the British Library

ISBN 978-1-009-59324-3 Hardback
ISBN 978-1-009-59322-9 Paperback
ISSN 2976-5684 (online)
ISSN 2976-5676 (print)

Cambridge University Press & Assessment has no responsibility for the persistence or accuracy of URLs for external or third-party internet websites referred to in this publication and does not guarantee that any content on such websites is, or will remain, accurate or appropriate.

For EU product safety concerns, contact us at Calle de José Abascal, 56, 1°, 28003 Madrid, Spain, or email eugpsr@cambridge.org

Hegel and Spinoza

Elements in the Philosophy of Georg Wilhelm Friedrich Hegel

DOI: 10.1017/9781009593205
First published online: January 2026

James Kreines
Claremont McKenna College
Author for correspondence: James Kreines, jkreines@cmc.edu

Abstract: This Element concerns Hegel's engagement with Spinoza's metaphysics, and is divided into three main parts. The first enlists help from Hegel's interpretation to introduce and defend philosophical strengths in Spinoza's defense of metaphysical monism. The second defends Hegel's criticism of Spinoza, concluding that Spinoza's philosophy must eliminate all finitude and determinacy, leaving only a shapeless abyss. The third employs these defenses to open up an approach to the philosophical interpretation of Hegel's Logic, the core of his philosophical system, understanding the meaning of Hegel's ambitious claims in terms of reasons that make them more than the mere unpacking of assumptions.

Keywords: Hegel, Spinoza, metaphysics, monism, absolute idealism

© James Kreines 2026

ISBNs: 9781009593243 (HB), 9781009593229 (PB), 9781009593205 (OC)
ISSNs: 2976-5684 (online), 2976-5676 (print)

Contents

0 Hegel and Spinoza: From Shapeless Abyss
   to Self-Developing Thought   1

1 Two Kinds of Reasons for Spinoza's Monism   13

2 The Abyss: Defense of Hegel's Immanent Critique   23

3 Hegel as Taking Metaphysics Seriously to Take it
   Dialectically: From Shapeless Abyss to Self-Developing
   Thought   41

   Sources   64

   References   66

0 Hegel and Spinoza: From Shapeless Abyss to Self-Developing Thought

§0.1 Hegel and Spinoza: Initial Images to Introduce the Chapters Below

Hegel sees the best aspects of Spinoza's metaphysics as containing something like an energy needed to get systematic philosophy going, to begin with a rough image.[1] But this energy, once it does get going, is supposed to ultimately send philosophy away from Spinoza, and in an entirely new kind of direction—Hegel's own. This is somehow supposed to be a kind of self-negation of Spinozism, on the way to a philosophy newly somehow centered on negation or self-negation. But making sense of this last idea is difficult, something to build towards; the way to approach it is to begin rather asking:

What is the Spinozist metaphysics that Hegel takes so seriously or thinks so important in this respect? Spinoza argues that there is only one substance, infinite and eternal, and that is all that there is.

Some might rather hold that reality is only a great disjointed heap of multiplicity, without organization or intelligibility. Spinoza argues for a very different view.

Some might hold that there is a transcendent God, responsible for freely creating a world. That requires at least two substances. Spinoza argues that there is only one. Spinoza sometimes calls his one substance "Nature," sometimes "God," and sometimes uses terms like: "the eternal and infinite being, whom we call God, or Nature" (E4Pref).

There being only one substance, itself infinite, is supposed to be compatible with you and me and our family members existing, even though we are many, and finite. To again give an image, which will need to be replaced with argument below, picture an ocean, with waves rolling across its surface. Multiplicity would come back to a one: many waves in one ocean. For the waves are not independently substantial. The waves just *are* the ocean: the ocean insofar as it sways or oscillates. So you and I would exist, but in a surprising and radically limited sense: merely like waves in an ocean. Spinoza's "substance monism" – the view that all there is is one substance – retains you and me as mere finite "modes" in, or "affections" of, the one substance.[2]

The core of Hegel's "abyss critique" of Spinoza (as I will call it) is to argue that Spinoza's own reasons, insofar as they could be reasons for the elimination of anything but one ocean – as it were – would also force elimination of all the

---

[1] Hegel is also unimpressed with other aspects of Spinozism, as noted below.
[2] On the wave image: Fleischman 1964, 10; Lin 2019: 112ff. I abstract for now from thought and extension as attributes of substance.

waves, or currents, or *any* determinate features of that ocean. That is to say, insofar as Spinoza has reasons for the elimination of any substances other than one infinite substance, these reasons would force the elimination of anything finite, of anything "in" substance, and of all determinate features of it. Spinoza's substance would be, Hegel says, "a shapeless abyss."[3]

I will argue that interpreters have not found and explained something essential by Hegel's own lights: how the argument provides reason against Spinoza's system, without begging the question. They again and again read Hegel in ways that leave him (whether they note this or not) merely presupposing something Spinoza argues against, or would naturally take himself to have argued against. I think we must solve this problem of a more substantial reason against Spinoza, if we are to hope to understand how Hegel uses Spinoza as a pivot toward a supposedly new form of philosophy.

Granted, some are already familiar with *terminology* expressing a sense of Hegel's critique and his alternative. Some might begin with: *Spinoza is a philosopher of the "affirmative"; Hegel takes this to be insufficient, revealing the need for a philosophy of "self-negation," or "absolute negation."*[4] But terminology like "absolute negation" is already familiar to interpreters, and yet they have again not (I argue) found the philosophical strength of Hegel's critique of Spinoza. Indeed we will see that a natural reading of the italicized interpretation would leave Hegel merely assuming some kind of negation antithetical to Spinoza, and so begging the question (§0.2; §2.2.2). For now, then, I seek to rest no weight on such terminology at the start, saving room to rethink and find the strength of the argument, earning my way back to terms like "absolute negation," or the contrast between our figures on this topic, providing in this sense more philosophical substance (§3.4).

Similarly, some might want me to begin by taking a side in debates about this topic, perhaps with something like: *Hegel's philosophy is a version of Spinoza's substance monism.* But many specialists would deny this, and some would even want to hear something more like: *Hegel pursues a kind of philosophy that does not take philosophically seriously the metaphysics of Spinoza's time, seeing it as outdated, naïve, extrinsic to the proper pursuit of philosophy.*[5] But these "sides"

---

[3] EL §151Zu, with other reference to "abyss" to follow.
[4] In Hegel, see e.g. SL 12:12, shortly before the guiding paragraph in the next section. On this theme, see e.g. Melamed (2012a).
[5] An example might be someone saying: Hegel thinks philosophy is reflection on the conditions of the possibility of determinate judgments about objects, and can address questions about objects themselves only in this light. Then Spinoza might seem naïve and not properly philosophical. But I think this would require philosophy to have from the start a distinction between judgments or a subject of judgment and objects themselves, and the beginning of the *Logic* is philosophical yet *without* such distinctions (§3.2).

exist, and yet the philosophical strength of Hegel's critique of Spinoza has not (I argue) been found. I try to avoid *assuming* either side-taking claim. I will *argue* that Hegel's philosophical reasoning only works by taking the metaphysics he sees in Spinoza as seriously as it can be taken; but in the most philosophically perspicacious sense, this will make his philosophy something other than just a version of Spinoza's substance monism.

I can now state the two large organizing aims of this book. The first is the defense of Hegel's "abyss critique." This organizes my first two chapters and requires a tight fit between them: §1 is on Spinoza's reasons for his monism, and §2 draws in part on this to show that *those very reasons* turn against Spinozism – in this way solving the problem that interpreters have not found Hegel's non-question-begging argument against Spinoza.

But there is another aim, which organizes all three chapters together. I argue that, insofar as interpreters have not found the philosophical strength of Hegel's Spinoza critique, this suggests that there is still much to learn about the problem of how reasons get themselves going in his new kind of systematic philosophy, in his *Science of Logic*, the core of his mature system. The problem of reasons in the *Logic* is harder: it is here that we get more general reasons against the general kinds of metaphysics of which Hegel sees Spinoza as just one example. So I conclude by drawing on results from the defense of the critique of Spinoza, and the general approach that sees Hegel as taking Spinoza's metaphysics seriously but critically, to propose an approach to that problem of: how reasons get going in the *Logic*, in a supposedly new way. I call the approach to Hegel's philosophy: taking metaphysics seriously to take it dialectically.[6]

§0.2 Tight Focus on Reasons, in an Open-Minded Sense

This section concerns a respect in which I will maintain the tight focus necessary for such a short book: the book is focused throughout on philosophical *reasons*, in a sense I will now explain.

I start with this point again: I think interpreters have not found the philosophical strength of Hegel's argument against Spinoza, in the specific sense that they read Hegel in ways that leave him (noted or not) *merely begging the question, or merely assuming something that Spinoza would naturally think he had already argued against.*

To explain what I mean with an example from far afield, if I argue that there are no universals, it would beg the question to say just: there are universals, so your argument fails. For all that is said, this assumes that there are universals,

---

[6] My use of terms here is not to distinguish "dialectical" from "speculative" moments and exclude the latter; I return to it most explicitly in §3.4.

and meets the argument with a mere assumption to the contrary. I think it is natural to say this is not yet any "reason" against the argument for universals.

My idea is that, while reasons in Spinoza and Hegel are hard to understand, we can start with a general sense of this philosophical lack or failure involved in begging the question, and take "reasons" in an open-minded sense, to be *anything* that we could come to understand as remedying the lack or failure. Or, take the term as initially empty of positive connotations beyond anything that would *not* merely beg the question. This will eventually lead us to entertain seriously Spinoza and Hegel's questioning of some natural-seeming assumptions about what reasons must be like, for example, that they must be reason*ing* from premises standing in a relation of grounding to a conclusion.[7] The point is *not* to pause here until it is understood how reasons might not be reasoning, in that sense; it is to begin with a paradigm of lack of reason, to help prepare an openness to later finding unexpected ways to fill that lack.

As thus defined, my sense of "reason" or "reasons" is not meant to capture usage in Spinoza or Hegel, but to orient toward adjudicating something between them.

My focus on reasons, in this sense, is not limited to Hegel's response to Spinoza. In general, and so including Spinoza, I focus tightly on interpreting philosophical works specifically in terms of the reasons animating them.

Why think this sense of "reason" relevant to Hegel? We can take up a guiding passage on Spinoza. It is found at a crucial juncture in Hegel's *Logic*: the transition away from a broader kind of metaphysics of which he takes Spinoza as exemplary, and to something meant to be newer. Hegel is clear that he rules out moving on in ways that just beg the question with respect to "Spinoza's system":

> ... refutation must not come from outside; that is, it must not proceed from assumptions which lie beyond that system and do not correspond with it. It only requires not to acknowledge those assumptions ...

For example, a "refutation" cannot "presuppose" – this passage tells us – "the freedom and independence of the self-conscious subject."[8] I think this is easy to understand: Spinoza's defense of his monism *argues* that everything is in some sense necessary, and in so doing *argues* against the reality of any freedom of the will incompatible with this.[9] If we say "I reject Spinozism because it is

---

[7] There is some reason to think Spinoza appeals to a contrasting form of immediacy (§1.2), and Hegel takes this seriously but critically (§3.2). Hegel himself thinks *if* "reasoning from grounds" (*Raisonnement aus Gründen*) was all there was, then this would be empty (SL 11:311); but it is not all: The core of reason is speculative-dialectical reason. Again, this is all to be understood later.

[8] The text here goes beyond, but includes my point.

[9] On necessity (E1P29), on free will (E1P32) vs. an accepted sense of freedom (E1D7).

incompatible with freedom of the will," and try to take this in itself as a philosophical reason against it, then I would merely assume that there is free will, and thus meet the argument with a mere assumption to the contrary. I find it easy to understand Hegel's insistence that this is something systematic philosophy "must not" do. So, Hegel himself insists on the importance of there being here something that does not beg the question, and that is just the sense of "reason" in my open-minded, initially merely negative sense.

In theory, one could try to defend free will in some other way and use this against Spinoza. But *Hegel* commits to something else, and something that takes Spinoza more seriously. He says:

> ... True refutation must engage the force of the opponent and must place itself within the compass of his strength ... (SL 12:15; JS 2:215)

Hegel commits to finding strength "within" Spinoza's metaphysics, and he claims to use that very strength against Spinoza – rather than some consideration from without, as it were.

Imagine then someone saying this: *Hegel rejects Spinoza's substance monism because it excludes some kind of Hegelian negation.* I would not say this, as the risk of confusion is too great. Spinoza argues for his metaphysics. If there is some sense of "negation" in which this is excluded, then we cannot give reason against Spinoza by merely assuming this incompatible negation.[10]

Certainly there are senses in which Hegel will *conclude* that Spinozism fails to do justice to negation, freedom, and much else besides. But Hegel commits to *reaching* that destination through his immanent engagement with the "strength" of Spinoza's philosophy. So nothing in the destination or any desire to reach it can serve as a "reason" against Spinoza. In our same guiding passage, this is part of the point here:

> ... the refutation of Spinoza's system can consist solely in this, that his standpoint be first recognized as essential and as necessary, but that secondly this standpoint be raised *out of itself* to a higher. (SL 12:15; JS 2:215)

We reach the supposedly "higher" "standpoint" of Hegel's philosophy specifically by recognizing and engaging "within the compass" of Spinoza's "strength."[11]

---

[10] It is widely recognized that such an appeal to Hegelian negation would violate Hegel's commitment here, even by those who think that Hegel does make such appeal, e.g. Parkinson 1977: 454; Bartuschat 2007: 111; Melamed 2012a: 187–88.

[11] There is much else to be said about the destination, and how things would look judged retrospectively. For example, in some sense the end of the *Logic* circles back to its beginning (SL 12:252). But this cannot provide the promised reason against Spinoza, through which one first gets to the end. Similarly, Hegel promises a reason *here* that could not be provided by a claim that Spinoza's philosophy will turn out later not a competitor but in some sense a "moment" of Hegel's; cf. Rödl 2018 on the lack of competition.

But there are also grounds to emphasize this sense of "reason" in Spinoza and Hegel, independent of the latter's critique of the former: For neither figure thinks that we can grasp the ultimate objects of their philosophical systems via perception or imagination. If not, then in what terms are we meant to grasp the objects of Spinoza's and Hegel's philosophies? Spinoza holds that, trying to infer *from* something finite *to* God – applying this form of reasoning is already a misunderstanding of what his "God, or nature" even is.[12] I take this to suggest that what God is requires understanding in terms of how something other than argument-from-the-finite animates the *Ethics*. And I certainly think that is Hegel's view in his case: we cannot grasp his "absolute idea" in the *Logic* until and unless grasping his unusual form of reasons. These are reasons that engage with positions – prominently including the kind of metaphysics of which Spinoza's is supposed to be exemplary – finding them "negating" themselves, and in this finding some kind of self-development of thought or its content. In some sense that is difficult to grasp in advance, the ultimate object of the *Logic* turns out just to *be* that process of "dialectical"/"speculative" reason or logic (§3.4).

But the point is again precisely *not* to delay here trying to understand dialectical-speculative logic, or "absolute idea". On the contrary, the point is to begin with *just* the paradigmatic *lack* of reason highlighted in our guiding passage forbidding question-begging. We can then use the term "reason" for *anything* that remedies this, seeking to understand Spinoza's and Hegel's philosophies in terms of the sometimes surprising reasons that animate them.

§0.3 Defense of Hegel's Critique of Spinoza: Into the Shapeless Abyss

This focus on reasons allows further introduction of the first organizing aim of the book: a new interpretation and defense of Hegel's abyss critique. Chapter 1 is an account of Spinoza's *reasons* for substance monism, with an assist from Hegel's view of them; this plays an essential role in Chapter 2's defense of Hegel's case that *these very reasons* actually undercut Spinoza's view, by forcing the conclusion that Spinoza's substance is a "dark, shapeless abyss, which swallows up into itself every determinate content as vacuous" (EL §151Zu).[13] Spinoza's reasons should force him to deny, to begin with, all reality to anything finite. For Spinoza, this would include denial of the existence of the "finite modes" supposedly "in" substance. Assuming we are finite, he would be forced to deny we exist *in any way at all*. He would be forced to deny central features of his own metaphysics.

---

[12] E2p10s2.   [13] See the note in §0.5 about the relation to "acosmism."

The key to finding the strength of Hegel's argument will be to understand a Hegelian distinction between two kinds of reasons potentially doing the work, in Spinoza, of supporting substance monism; that is the topic of §1.

One kind of reason (§1.1) is initially more approachable. We easily reason from a broken window to the cause on which it depends: impact of the baseball. Such reasoning involves causation, one form of what we can more generally call *explanatory dependence*, or *priority-involving dependence*: we think of the impact as prior in causing the break, and not being caused by the break. In Hegel's terms, this is a sense in which the break would be "mediated" by the impact.

What brings Spinoza to the center of debate at Hegel's time is the idea that popular philosophy uses such easy forms of dependence-based reasoning, but in an *ad hoc* or unprincipled manner. Spinoza, by contrast, is supposed to provide a way of being consistent about mediation. *Very* roughly, as a start, being consistent and principled about causal reasoning is supposed to support determinism, and in this way put pressure on the forms of freedom of the will that Spinoza denies.[14]

Hegel sees a second kind of reason suggested in Spinoza, and while it is difficult to come to see how this could be a form of reason, the attribution is at least familiar in some Spinoza scholarship (§1.2). The idea here would be of Spinoza as drawing our attention to some kind of intellectual and *immediate* grasp of the existence of the infinite substance, or God – not needing reason*ing* in dependence on, or mediation by, established premises.[15]

The distinction, then, is between reasons of mediation and immediacy. We will see that it corresponds to the distinction between the topics of the first two of three parts of Hegel's *Logic*, the first concerned with immediacy, and the second with mediation. In a sense, Hegel's own explanation of how his critiques of immediacy and mediation combine is the *Logic*. But we begin with Hegel's many references to (and criticisms of) Spinoza, many of which are found in those two parts, focusing on Spinoza *considered as resting monism on immediacy*, and then Spinoza *considered as consistently thinking through mediation*.

I will not argue that Spinoza really rests the weight on immediacy as a reason, nor the claim that this immediacy could really serve as a real reason for substance monism. There is no need. §2 will defend Hegel's criticism by arguing that, to whatever degree Spinoza's case rests weight here, *or* on

---

[14] This is part of Jacobi's idea in 1785, along with the more radical insistence that this is *the* guiding thread throughout the *Ethics*; I defend the philosophy side of this in my 2025a and 2025b.

[15] In Spinoza scholarship, Garrett (2018: 57) and on *scientia intuitiva* (2018, 209), following up Earle (1973) and Wolfson (1934).

mediation, *or* some combination, he would and should regardless be forced (as Hegel alleges) to conclude that substance is merely an indeterminate abyss.

Another key here will be to remain consistently focused on taking Spinoza's *reasons* seriously. As we will see, some (not all) interpreters claim to defend Spinoza by pointing out that he does not think substance is an abyss; he commits, for example, to the reality of finite modes. But this is so far from being any defense against the abyss critique that it is actually *part* of the critique! The point is the internal conflict of Spinoza's *reasons* for monism forcing him, *against his intention*, to eliminate finite modes and all determinacy in substance.

Ironically, precisely those who fail to see the philosophical strengths in Spinoza's metaphysics – those who think they are somehow beyond such metaphysics – must miss the philosophical force of Hegel's critique, and consequently its importance to him. It is only by finding strengths in Spinoza's reasons that Hegel can hope to turn them against Spinoza.

The real unnoticed key, however, is how the distinction of two kinds of reasons highlights two strands of critique. Given one strand alone, it will seem to leave ways to defend Spinoza. But interpreters have missed the ways in which their defenses against one strand will give force to another side of the critique that they missed. It is the combination of strands that will be so strong in critique of Spinoza (§2.3).

In a sense, one organizing aim of the book should be complete at this point. The very reasons for Spinoza's monism (§1) leave substance a shapeless abyss (§2).

§0.4 Hegel as Taking Metaphysics Seriously but Dialectically: To Self-Determining Thought

How might understanding Hegel's engagement with the kinds of metaphysics he sees in Spinoza contribute to an understanding of how reasons get themselves going at the start of Hegel's own project in theoretical philosophy, his *Science of Logic*, in some new and distinctively Hegelian manner? I think my just-summarized results, in the first two chapters, will make it natural to suspect that there is more to learn in response to this problem, and more difficulties to be faced; and also make it natural to suspect defense of the abyss critique can help to that end. Why is this natural? I would explain in three steps:

First, the issues arising with the kinds of metaphysics Hegel sees in Spinoza seem to be wired into the structure of the *Logic*. The guiding passage above, for example, concerns immanent critique of Spinoza and occurs at a crucial transition to the final part of the book. Furthermore, as we will see, the *Logic* begins and gets its reasoning going with discussion of *indeterminacy* – the kind of position to which he thinks Spinoza is pushed, with added commentary here on Spinoza.[16] Finally, Hegel's case that thought of Spinoza turns against itself, contradicts itself, or negates itself is an example of the "dialectic" that will also structure the *Logic*. He says, for example:

> The realization that the dialectic makes up the very nature of thinking and that as understanding it is bound to land in the negative of itself, i.e. in contradiction, constitutes a cardinal aspect of logic. (§11An).

Second, interpreters have again not solved the problems of reasons (in the sense of Hegel's prohibition of begging the question) in his immanent critique of Spinoza.

Third, the problem of reasons animating the *Logic* is similar, but more difficult. The *Logic* begins with immediacy. Roughly, Hegel thinks a beginning is precisely something not *mediated* by prior steps. And the *Logic* finds reason here to think that such immediacy forces elimination of determinacy. In the engagement *specifically with Spinoza*, this is enough: Spinoza is deeply committed to the determinacy of finite modes, and so we would have an internal conflict. But to get reasons moving in the *Logic,* this is not enough. For the issue here is a reason why it is proper to the metaphysics of immediacy to *embrace* indeterminacy, as Hegel thinks is the case with Parmenides. Could we reject this on grounds that there is or should be determinacy? That would presuppose something begging the question, by the standards of the reasoning or thinking of the *Logic*. So the challenge of reason or non-question-begging thinking in the *Logic* is greater.

I therefore think it natural to see interpreters' not finding the strength of the reasons in the critique of Spinoza to suggest that there is still much to learn in the more difficult case of finding reasons animating the *Logic*. And to suggest that defense of the abyss critique in the face of this kind of problem might help with the broader issues of the *Logic*.

Granted, the whole of Hegel's *Logic* and the whole system is in almost every sense beyond the scope of this small book. What I mean to do in my third chapter is just to propose and initiate an interpretative approach, allowing space constraints to impose a number of limitations. For example, I bring to bear only the specific results concerning Spinoza, and the general seriously/dialectically approach. And I interpret in detail only at the beginning of the first part of the *Logic* ("Being"), on immanent critique of immediacy, and on the immediacy reason to eliminate determinacy, to try to understand how Hegelian reasons can

---

[16] As well as Parmenides, for example, to whose position Hegel argues Spinoza is pushed.

get moving in the first place in the *Logic*. There will be space then only to show that this interpretation does not foreclose, but opens space for approaching the other junctures in the *Logic*'s broadest three-part structure: a second part ("Essence") focused on mediation; and a third part ("The Concept") ending up with something supposed to be new.

I again call the approach I propose here: Hegel as taking metaphysics seriously, but to take it dialectically. I mean specifically: the metaphysics of immediacy and mediation, which Hegel finds throughout the history of Western philosophy.

I am carefully saying that I will propose and initiate this seriously/dialectically approach, arguing for the *promise* of this in addressing difficulties in the *Logic*. My point is not to express personal reservations about the approach; other parts of the defense of the approach are continuing to appear in my other work on Hegel and classical German philosophy.[17] My point is that one chapter of a small book can only be a small part of that extended defense.

§0.5 Last First Notes

In §1, I seek the strengths in Spinoza's reasons for his monism. I do not imagine that *all* readers will give up *all* hope of any counter-argument. Indeed, I will also defend (§2) the strengths of Hegel's reasons against Spinoza. I do not seek to portray Hegel as somehow beyond all possible counter-argument. The standard of success in this kind of history of philosophy is to find, in anything worth considering at length, reasons strong enough to learn from, philosophically speaking. Compare Hegel on Spinoza: he sees weaker points and stronger points; he focuses (wisely, in my view) on the stronger points, the ones from which philosophy has the most to learn.

In this way we can take Spinoza and Hegel seriously, without having to try to pretend to declare a final victor beyond any possible challenge, and also without making one seem the same as the other.

Some might object that *Hegel's* kind of reasons are supposed to be somehow absolutely decisive. But I think it is difficult enough, and a good first step, to approach by trying (as I do here) to get some sense of how they could be reasons at all.

I do not take my focus on reasons to conflict with the need to understand philosophers in their historical context. It is one essential and philosophical way of doing that: understanding philosophers in terms of the reasons with which they engage their past and contemporaries.[18]

---

[17] On Hegel, beginning with my 2020.
[18] I give elsewhere complimentary accounts of Hegel's context and figures important to Hegel: Kant (2015); Jacobi (2025a); and German Idealism generally (2025a, 2025b).

In focusing on reasons animating forms of philosophy that are distant – historically and/or culturally – I seek to avoid assuming that this requires or would mean portraying them as similar to anything popular in journals of philosophy here and now. I would not defend Hegelianism by saying, for example: don't worry, it is more like an account of the normativity of meaning than anything more distant or unfamiliar today. I would apply the same approach not just to Spinoza and Hegel but also to the forms of Buddhist philosophy mentioned by Hegel and briefly below (§3.2.1). This commitment is not antiquarianism. It is the opposite. The point is to look to distant philosophy to contribute to forward-looking expansion of the perspective of today. Engagement across difference contributes to forward progress, and it is lost if we reduce distant philosophy to the recently popular.

There is no space here for interesting forms of system-critical responses to Spinoza and Hegel, from Jacobi to Kierkegaard, Adorno, and so on. But part of my aim here is to help in the appreciation of this, by arguing that there are extreme forms of systematicity in Spinoza and Hegel that are philosophically *worth* the engagement given to them in such system-critical philosophy.[19]

This book would be misunderstood if read as trying to cohere with everything in my *Reason in the World* (2015): that book now seems to me too deflationary on some points, and (not unrelated) insufficiently attentive to the importance of Spinoza.[20]

Similarly, this book would be misunderstood if taken to pursue my old argument (2006) against what was then called the "non-metaphysical" Hegel, arguing its proponents should and would drop that idea, turning to advance their new approaches as forms of metaphysics. I think this already happened. As to *pre-critical* metaphysics, I briefly return to implications about this in §3.4.

By Hegel's *Logic*, I mean here both the self-standing *Science of Logic* (SL); and "First Part: The Science of Logic" (EL) of the *Encyclopedia*. My priority is the SL. I use "Hegel," unless noted, to refer to the mature Hegel, by which I mean the period beginning with publication of first parts of the SL (1812) through Hegel's death. I try to rest on continuities during this time, even if there are also differences that would be important to other kinds of studies.

---

[19] I have defended Jacobi's system-critique in this way in my 2025a.
[20] I'm especially indebted for responses from Brady Bowman, Franz Knappik, Jake McNulty, and Clinton Tolley.

In stating my tight focus points above, I mean as well that my focus is *not* covering everything in Spinoza's *Ethics,* in Hegel or his *Logic,* or everything that Hegel has to say about Spinoza; comprehensive intellectual influences; Hegel's work earlier than 1812 or his development; what Hegel's engagement with Spinoza leads him to concerning topics like human freedom, religion, etc. I hope this short book is also of use to those who would focus elsewhere.

1 Two Kinds of Reasons for Spinoza's Monism

In this chapter, I distinguish two kinds of reasons suggested in Spinoza's case for monism, along the lines of Hegel's distinction between immediacy and mediation as topics for the first two parts of Hegel's *Logic*. I begin with reasons of mediation or dependence (§1.1), and then turn to immediacy (§1.2). The importance of this is *not* to pretend to establish Spinozist conclusions, to then take them as given as premises that Hegel would use to ground or justify some extension or modification of Spinoza; it is rather to prepare for Hegel to find the reasons animating substance monism to turn against themselves, so that substance monism destroys itself, as it were. But precisely given this, these details of Spinoza's serious reasons are needed for any philosophically serious attempt to make Hegel's critique stick; it is not at all Hegelian to think oneself instead immediately beyond such metaphysics: one must take it seriously to take it dialectically.

§1.1 Mediation in Spinoza's Case for Monism

1.1.1 Mediation in the Sense of Dependence, as an Organizing Thread

I begin by introducing a kind of mediation or dependence-oriented reason, before looking in this light at the ontological scheme and initial demonstrations of the *Ethics*.

One might think initially that the geometric form of the *Ethics* lays out all the reasons to easily see, each proposition demonstrated with reference to prior elements, beginning with axioms and definitions. So why ask about Spinoza's reasons? But we will see that interpreters – from Hegel to our contemporaries – tend to seek simpler common thread(s), organizing the whole, providing philosophical strength.

Hegel himself finds the geometric form in itself misleading, at best. He sees it as, in itself, compatible with an arbitrary choice of definitions and axioms, which would beg the question in philosophical disputes.[21] Hegel quickly dismisses many using this method.[22] But he finds another spirit in Spinoza – a common thread or threads – lending philosophical strength. That's why he thinks Spinozism cannot be simply brushed aside on grounds of the geometric form, or anything else, but requires using its own strengths against it.[23]

As noted above, the initially more approachable kind of reason turns on consideration of forms of dependence, including causality and grounding – all of which Hegel collects under the heading of "mediation."

---

[21] VGP 3:263.
[22] Hegel sees little of specifically philosophical interest in Wolff, whose use of this method is said to be pedantic (3:348ff./20:256ff.).
[23] On Jacobi here Sandkaulen, e.g. 2000: 93f.

The general idea of a Spinoza of mediation – common in Hegel's context, due to F. H. Jacobi – is that a common thread in Spinoza's case for monism, lending strength, can be approached in this way: Spinoza exposes popular philosophies of the time as *ad hoc* in their appeals to such dependence, seeking to protect common sense about things like free will. Spinoza's strength would be rather thinking through forms of dependence more consistently.

One way in which the *Ethics* draws on conceptions of dependence, much discussed recently, is in stating and using a "principle of sufficient reason" (PSR). There can be different versions of the PSR. One clear one in the *Ethics* is: "[f]or each thing there must be assigned a cause, *or* reason (*causa seu ratio*), both for its existence and for its nonexistence" (E1P11D2). Striking here is the bi-directionality: not just existence but also non-existence depends on a cause or reason. Call this "Bi-PSR." Whatever else we say about this, Spinoza does state it, and uses it in demonstrations about God leading up to his monism (again beginning with E1P11D2).

Spinoza also refers to the common "nihilo" form of PSR: nothing comes from or is produced by nothing (*ex nihilo nihil fit*) (e.g. E4P20S; cf. Short Treatise at CW 66). This expresses the existence side of Bi-PSR: something existing must come from something, that is, have a cause or ground.[24] Descartes' *Meditations* uses a similar statement in its causal proof of God.

There is a radical Jacobi *subvariety* of the Spinoza of mediation, which I neither assume nor need here. This is to argue that the PSR specifically is *the* common thread throughout the whole case for Spinoza's monism. So Jacobi says other philosophers are *ad hoc* in use of the *nihilo*-PSR, but the "spirit" of Spinoza is to carry specifically this through most consistently.[25]

Something along those lines, but not always so extreme, is important in the flourishing of philosophical work on Spinoza in recent decades: the idea that the PSR is at least *one* unifying and strengthening thread throughout the *Ethics*. An important and seminal text in this work is Garrett's argument on this score in his 1979 "Spinoza's Ontological Argument." Garrett's recent book tells us early on what we need "to understand the system that Spinoza proposes," and begins with a PSR as one guiding thread, demanding a cause or reason for *every* fact (2018: 13). If there are other facts aside from those concerning existence and non-existence, this might go farther still; I'll call it a "fact-PSR."

---

[24] CW I/20–1, 66–8; (I/83); Letter 10/196.
[25] E.g. JWA 1–57/205. I note that Jacobi also rejects Spinozism, but there is no room to consider his anti-systematic turn here. I have said more about Jacobi's influence on Hegel in my 2025b.

Della Rocca has more recently identified Jacobi as an influence, and argued for the more radical view that the fact-PSR is *the* guiding thread or spirit throughout.[26]

But Hegel's interest in a Spinoza of mediation is broader. It is not limited to a focus on "ground" (*Grund*) in a PSR or "Satz des Grundes" (e.g. GW §121An), and Hegel treats Spinoza as thinking through many dependence relations in a principled manner. I will try to note as I proceed how this approach might differ from the idea that the PSR specifically is driving arguments throughout the whole of the *Ethics*. I don't mean to settle that interpretive issue about Spinoza, but to show that Hegel does not *depend* on anything as radical as Jacobi: Hegel could allow but does not need attribution of *fact*-PSR to the *Ethics* (as opposed to the Bi-PSR and nihilo, explicit in the text), nor attributing *any* PSR as *the single* guiding thread, nor thinking the *Ethics* reasons *from the start* via a PSR.

Now I turn to the beginning of the *Ethics*, looking to consideration of dependence relations as providing strength. I will note some difficult spots that would make more difficult and lengthy a defense *all the way to substance monism*. But targeting those spots would not show his argument going wrong *in a way that could save* commonsense belief that you and I are substances, unlike mere waves in an ocean. Or so I argue.

1.1.2 Spinoza's Ontological Scheme

On Hegel's view, as far as the geometric form itself tells us, Spinoza's axioms and definitions could be merely arbitrary. I seek to introduce the definitions and axioms important here in a way that opens the possibility that hard-to-resist thoughts about dependence might unify Spinoza's ontological scheme and lend strength downstream.

We can begin with the "modes," also known as "affections." Some popular illustrations: a wave, a dent, a smile.[27] I take it that Spinoza's idea here is not merely arbitrary, but a difficult-to-resist thought about dependence: the wave is the ocean, insofar as it is oscillating. To *conceive* of what a wave is would be to grasp that it is not independent, but *in* another. In general, a mode or affection is "conceived through" this dependence on something else, being "in" that something else. That is the latter part of the definition of mode:

> By mode I mean the affections of substance, that is, that which is in something else and is conceived through something else. (E1D5)

---
[26] (Della Rocca 2015: 524). Garrett pushes for a smaller role for the PSR (Garrett 2018, ch. 2 postscript).
[27] E.g. (van Cleve 1999: 157); (Lin 2019: 112–15).

The first part refers to substance. Spinoza needs no mere *assumption* that there is any substance; he later gives reason. But to be substance *would* be, first, to be independent in this sense, or to *not* be conceived through another.

Commonsense examples of substances are not appropriate, since Spinoza is arguing that all that we ordinarily think is substantial – e.g. you and I – is not.

Spinoza's definition of substance is not framed negatively, saying a substance is something *not* conceived through something else. Rather, it says that substance *is* conceived through itself. Spinoza sees no gap. I think the idea is this: for everything that is, there must be something to it, in the sense of something that would be grasped, in grasping what it is. In this sense, everything would be in principle (if perhaps not in practice, or by me) "conceivable." We can see this in the second axiom:

> E1A2. That which cannot be conceived through another thing must be conceived through itself.

This gives an initial sense of why Spinoza thinks – and this will be important downstream – that his ontological scheme is *exhaustive*: if there is something not conceivable through itself (substance), then it is conceivable through another (a mode).

The story is parallel about dependence in the sense of being "in" something, but I will just note it. The parallel axiom is:

> E1A1. All things that are, are either in themselves or in something else.

In some sense, substance is in itself.[28]

And so the definition of substance begins by rolling together the considerations of my last few paragraphs:

> By substance I mean that which is in itself and is conceived through itself... (E1D3)

One of Spinoza's later statements of the exhaustiveness of his ontological scheme refers to these very definitions and axiom: "nothing exists but substance and its modes (Ax. I and Defs. 3 and 5)" (E1P28D).

In the ontological scheme, it remains to define "attribute." There are complexities here, but the only thing we need in this chapter is a sense in which an attribute is the *essence* of substance. I would explain it in this way: Descartes thinks his own mind is a finite substance. What explains the possibility of his

---

[28] I try to avoid making anything downstream on interpretation of this part.

mind being affected, in the sense of thinking about Napoleon? Not just that it is a *thing*: it seems conceivable that there are things that cannot think at all. Rather, that it is a *thinking thing*. Or: that there is a *substance* with the attribute *thought*. So, the attribute explains the possibility of all the ways the substance can be affected: it is that on which all those ways *depend*. And, in this, *nothing comes between substance and attribute*, or – roughly – the essence of substance, and substance. So, this does not violate exhaustiveness: if something is not substance (conceived through itself in terms of attribute or essence), it is mode or affection.

The definition of attribute is more complex:

> By attribute I mean that which the intellect perceives of substance as constituting its essence. (E1D4)

The complexities about the intellect seem related to the issue of whether one substance can have *multiple* attributes (§2.1.3). This is a difficult spot, to be sure. But it does not matter to the argument defended in this chapter: it cannot block the initial steps towards monism in a way that would save the commonsense that you and I are more substantial than affections. *These* steps assume nothing about any possibility or account of multiple attributes of a substance.

1.1.3 Demonstrations: Substance is Uncaused; You and I are not Substances

I want to first follow in more detail Spinoza's argument that substance must be uncaused, along these lines:

[S1] Two substances cannot share an attribute.

[S2] Substances without a shared attribute cannot have causal relations.

[S3] One substance cannot cause another to exist. (from [S1], [S2])

We can start with [S1]. Hegel thinks this is obvious from the definitions (VGP 265/Mich. 879). Spinoza offers more detail as to why: E1P4 makes a requirement on any case of distinct things (*numerically* distinct, which is how I will use "distinct" unless noted). For any two distinct things, something must distinguish them. We can approach the general requirement in terms reminiscent of explanations above: for there to be a numerical distinction, there would have to be something to it, such that one would grasp that something in grasping them as distinct. Initially it might seem that one wave, for example, could be distinct from another in having a different shape.

Let me note two ways of thinking of this, without need here to settle the matter. Some see this requirement on distinctness as implied by the fact-PSR, and the fact that one thing is distinct from another.[29]

Here is an optional alternative: We could just focus directly on the claim that *distinctness depends on distinguishers*. This approach would say that the claim is clear and convincing on its own, and more so than something so general or sweeping as the fact-PSR, which then would not be needed to do work at this early point. This approach could still find strength in Spinoza's consistency in this kind of appeal to dependence as he proceeds. This might include later (E1P1D2) explicit appeal to Bi-PSR in the cases of existence and non-existence. But one need not see Spinoza's earlier demonstrations as from that principle.

In any case, if distinctness depends on something, then Spinoza's exhaustive ontological scheme allows only either an attribute (implied, an attribute/substance pair), or else modes or affections (E1P4).

So, could a sphere and a cube be numerically distinct merely or only in virtue of differing shapes? Note that these features cannot be attributes: the possibility of being a sphere is dependent on, explained by, something else, namely, being *extended* – so extension would be the attribute that explains the possibility of being so affected. We are considering, then, the possibility that mere affections could distinguish substances. I think the general point is that an affection of a substance just is the substance, insofar as so affected. So, if we are told only of two different affections, we don't yet know *what it is* that is so affected. And we would have to know *what* we are dealing with to ground one of them not being another. So, "if they are distinguished by a difference of affections … there cannot be several such substances but only one" (E1P5).

Now Spinoza's version of this conclusion involves another difficult spot: he concludes that no two substances can share an attribute. Some think it follows only that attributes must in some way distinguish substances, allowing *partially* overlapping sets of attributes.[30] I come back to this to show it does not matter to the early steps towards monism, or block them in a way saving commonsense about our being finite substances.

<u>Substance as uncaused</u>: [S2] is independent of [S1], arguing that causal interaction between substances would require a shared attribute.

Consider this as about dependence: If substances interact, this would depend on something that explains the possibility of interaction. But extension and thought are attributes, so there is nothing beneath them, as it were, on which to depend. For example, in Princess Elisabeth's famous worry about

---

[29] Della Rocca (2008: 47); Lin objects (2019: 45f).

[30] Della Rocca 2008: 49ff.; I come back at the end of this section.

Descartes: why my mind affects my body rather than yours cannot depend on contact, as this is specific to extension. Now, say we do find something through which to explain the interaction between a mind and a body. But then we seem to have found that thought and extension are not attributes: there is something beneath them, closer to substance, through which to explain interaction of thinking and extended things. Either way, we can see why Spinoza concludes that:

> E1P2. Two substances having different attributes have nothing in common.
> E1P3. When things have nothing in common, one cannot be the cause of the other.

In a letter, Spinoza connects the *nihilo* PSR: "for since there would be nothing in the effect which it had in common with the cause, whatever the effect had, it would have from nothing" (CW 1–172; Letter 4). But, again, we could take this point to stand best on its own, and then contribute to a broader consistent way of dealing with dependence, including later use of the PSR.

In sum, [S2], substances cannot share attributes; [S1], causal relations require a shared attribute; So, [S3]: "One substance cannot be produced by another substance" (E1P6). Thus, substances cannot be caused to exist.

Now, consider you and me. We both seem to have causes of our existence. And we seem to interact: you are reading something I wrote. If so, then we would be mere affections, conceived through one common substance; in this, like waves in an ocean.[31]

Glimpsing monism: This concludes the steps towards monism that I defend and claim rule out objections from commonsense; but I will briefly gesture at the next steps. Spinoza next (E1P7) claims that substance has existence in its nature, or is self-caused or a *causa sui* in this sense, as defined at the start (E1D1). Perhaps this follows from PSR-based reasoning (Garrett 1979, 205).

Spinoza then notes that, to be finite would require something greater of the same nature, or a limit in this respect (E1D2). He claims it follows that (E1P8) substance must be infinite; Hegel explains:

> ... otherwise it must be limited by another substance of the same nature, in which case there would be two substances of the same attribute, which is contrary to the fifth proposition.[32]

---

[31] If concerned that "in" might not follow from "conceived through," I think the latter is the challenge to commonsense; it does seem commonsense that we interact at least in part through being "in" something like a universe with an attribute of extension.

[32] (VGP 3:265/Mich. 879). I don't think the complexity about a *conceivably* greater matters here.

Still the case for monism is not complete: If Spinoza allows multiple attributes, he has not ruled out there being *many* substances, each infinite within a different attribute. This matters little for us: it would not save commonsense about ourselves as finite substance; and Hegel's rejoinder below (§2) would force all such substances to be wholly indeterminate, eliminating all finitude. So I do not dwell on it.

But, in brief, the definition of God is:

> By God I mean an absolutely infinite being, that is, substance consisting of infinite attributes, each of which expresses eternal and infinite essence. (E1D6)

Spinoza is going to try to argue via the Bi-PSR, and a case for the impossibility of any cause or ground of God's non-existence. And if there cannot be attribute sharing, all other substances are ruled out.[33]

Against commonsense rejoinders: While there is no space to defend those further steps to monism, they are not needed to counter the resistance I find most common: someone finds it objectionably contrary to commonsense to think of themselves as a mere affection. They see this as reason to suspect Spinoza's argument fails. And they see that there are some difficult spots in the whole argument for monism, some noted above. So, they wish to reject Spinoza's metaphysics in favor of commonsense.

But we have seen enough to rebuff this: Say we go all the way back to an early difficult spot: Perhaps substances *can* share attributes, as long as they *also* have differentiating attributes. But how would this allow us to maintain a commonsense view that you and I are substances? If commonsense is the point, then it will be maintained that you and I and billions of others can interact. So we would all need to share attributes (perhaps, extension and thought), and yet each have at least one attribute that all others lack. This would require billions of fundamental attributes of which no one has any inkling at all, distributed in just the right manner and no other.

I take it *Spinoza's* worry here would be that there is nothing to explain why just one person would have a given unknown attribute, and everyone else lack it.[34] But here I will just say that this picture is at best no more commonsense about what we are than Spinoza's. Similarly, even if Spinoza cannot rule out multiple infinite substances, he would have ruled out our being substances. So I think I have defended Spinoza's argument for monism far enough to rule out challenges to monism motivated by such commonsense. Fortunately, *Hegel* plans something else: immanent critique.

---

[33] Actually, infinite attributes, but I put off this complexity to §2.1.2–3.
[34] Again, Della Rocca 2008: 49ff.

§1.2 An Immediacy Reason in Spinoza?

Hegel, along with many Spinoza interpreters, sees another kind of reason suggested in Spinoza as well: nothing to do with a PSR or any kind of mediation or dependence, but rather a kind of immediate reason.[35] It is not necessary for my purposes to settle whether Spinoza makes such an appeal in the *Ethics*. Nor to convince readers that this immediacy really is a form of *reason*—a way of not begging the question. Here it is only important to be familiar enough with the idea to be ready for my later case that an immediacy reason for Spinoza's monism would force substance to be an abyss (§2.2); and for Hegel's critique of immediacy in his account of "being" (§3.2).

To introduce the idea, say we had a claim mentioned earlier: "[e]xistence belongs to the nature of substance" (E1P7). Or: "God's existence and his essence are one and the same" (E1P20). If so, then in grasping *what* substance is – or, in the second case, what God is – we would *already, immediately* grasp *that it exists*. No mediation by steps of argument, syllogism or demonstration needed.[36]

Sometimes interpreters borrow a term for this from Kant and post-Kantians: intellectual intuition. "Intuition" here, for Kant, requires immediacy.[37] For example, Earle refers in interpreting Spinoza to "an intellectual intuition of Substance" (1973: 223). Garrett: "intellectual intuition of God's existence" (2018: 57).

Sometimes interpreters refer to this as a kind of "ontological argument" (hereafter OA). This requires great care: Reference to a traditional theistic proof can seem to suggest traditional features of God, which Spinoza *opposes:* God as having free will, for example. And it can suggest classic formulations as a syllogism, also suggested by the very label "argument" (or "proof"). But that is contrary to the idea here. Say someone thought to begin an argument with something like "substance is F," or "God is F," and then argue from there to existence. But the form of such argument, or a syllogism, suggests that a first premise should be graspable independently of accepting the conclusion. The idea here, by contrast, is that we cannot grasp substance, or else God, without *already* grasping that it *is* or exists. Maybe a syllogistic formulation could serve

---

[35] This section is especially indebted to discussion with Kevin Harrelson, Jake McNulty, and Alex Host.

[36] If we distinguish the epistemic and the metaphysical, we might take this so far as a kind of epistemological immediacy: something would be *grasped* immediately. But Hegel's abyss critique effectively argues (§3.2) that these are two sides of one coin: something for which an immediate reason could be given would have to be something whose very nature is to be simple, immediate, e.g. independent of any parts or compound notions... and then as well something entirely indeterminate.

[37] Intellectual intuition "would grasp and present the object immediately and all at once" (Ak 8:389).

some purpose as approximation, but the immediacy reason would *not* be fundamentally syllogistic. If comparison to an OA is necessary, we should say 'immediacy-OA'.[38]

Perhaps such immediacy is suggested by Spinoza, in the course of the broader argument for monism, in the first demonstration of God's existence:

> ... conceive, if you can, that God does not exist. Therefore ... his essence does not involve existence. But this is absurd (Pr. 7). Therefore, God necessarily exists. (E1P11D1)

Garrett says this:

> ... allows Spinoza to urge his readers to *try for themselves* the experiment of seeking to conceive of God as not existing – an attempt that, if Spinoza is right, will lead the reader, in its failure, to experience *instead* the intellectual intuition of God's existence in the ontological argument. (2018: 57)[39]

(A terminological note: I think such intellectual intuition would be supposed to be a form of "reason" *in my sense here* – a way of revealing access to God that is (supposedly) *not* a mere arbitrary assumption that might then beg the question. *If* we take "reason" to *just* name a mediation relation between a premise and conclusion, then we must carefully use "intuition" to *contrast* with this; but that is not my usage here. Something more complicated is going on in Spinoza's contrast between his highest form of cognition, *scientia intuitiva,* and the adequate but only second-best *ratio* ("reason"). But my terminology is not meant to capture his *ratio*.)

The comparison to an OA does greatly help the understanding of something important to Hegel in Spinoza. Leibniz later worries that an OA raises the concern that the concept of God contains a "hidden contradiction."[40] Take the concept of a *number exceeded by no other.* In this case, we have the complexity of *number* and then in addition a negation like: *not exceeded*. We should then worry that these elements contradict one another, and immediately establish *non*-existence. So there seems to be a concern for any OA focused on any idea of God that is complex and involving negation, such as: *a being than which no greater can be conceived.*

It is striking in this light, and very important for Hegel, that Spinoza's idea of God is diametrically opposed: *he denies that God involves negation.* Spinoza explains the definition of God, referring to infinite attributes, saying that what

---

[38] See Harrelson (2009) on an "intuitive" OA, from the perspective of which "[a]ny ontological syllogism is inherently misleading" (2009: 88).

[39] On the one hand, the citation of E1P7 might this depend on a PSR demonstration and mediation? On the other, E1P8S2 suggests the point could be an axiom, present *immediately* at the start. See Host (2021: 29).

[40] Leibniz 1989: 238.

"belongs to the essence" of God is "whatever expresses essence and does not involve any negation" (E1D6E).[41] For example, to think instead of God in terms of free will, stopping short of a necessary nature necessitating everything, improperly "involves negation of power" (E2P3S). Not only *does* Spinoza deny that God involves negation, but we see here that – *if* an appeal to immediate grasp of God plays some role – his reasons *require* it. This will be important for defense of Hegel's critique (§2.2).

Note that my point here does not require arguing that no one could ever have an immediate, intuitive grasp of a God that is complex and involves negation. That would be harder, I would think. The point here is just that this would still be ill-fit to be offered as a reason, in the sense that I am attending here: imagine someone not yet convinced, against whom we must not beg the question. They should worry about hidden contradictions. One could address them with the *steps of an argument* that there is no hidden contradiction in one's complex and negation-involving idea of God. But this would shift the weight from immediacy to a conclusion mediated by the steps of that argument.

In sum, perhaps Spinoza appeals to an immediate grasp of God or substance, and perhaps this is meant to play some role in convincing us of his monism. If so, then this would require what Spinoza does in any case offer: an account of God as fully affirmative, or involving no negation.

Then again, perhaps the weight is meant to be carried at the end of the day rather by reasons of mediation, discussed above. I turn to show that Hegel's abyss critique applies to whatever reasons of immediacy and/or mediation might be meant by Spinoza to animate substance monism.

2 The Abyss: Defense of Hegel's Immanent Critique

As we have seen, Hegel promises immanent critique of Spinoza. The critique I defend in this chapter, and argue is so important for Hegel's own philosophy in the next, is again what I call the "abyss critique": Spinoza's substance is only a "shapeless abyss, as it were, that swallows up into itself every determinate content . . . ."[42]

What is the "determinateness" (*Bestimmtheit*, as Hegel usually puts it) that Spinoza must eliminate? One case is the finite (for Spinoza, finite modes). I will give Hegel's argument that Spinoza must, contrary to his intention, deny all reality to the finite – and this I will defend in detail.[43]

---

[41] Cf. Leibniz: "Nothing can prevent the possibility of what is without limits, without negation, and consequently without contradiction" (1989: 218).
[42] (§151Zu; GW 23,3:924)   [43] E.g. VGP 20:195/3:281/9:111/30,3:1282.

Another case would be Spinoza's infinite attributes of God. Given complexities concerning their interpretation, no full defense will fit here. But I argue that we can get a sense of why Hegel thinks Spinoza should be forced to deny any distinction between attributes, eliminating determinacy in this form as well.

I think elimination of finite modes is enough of an internal problem for Spinoza's substance monism – that this doctrine is intimately connected with the idea of finite modes *in* substance. Spinoza's *Ethics* speaks of there being finite things, and argues that there is an infinite regress of them in God (E1P28).[44]

Some defenses of Spinoza seem to me to leave him without reasons for his monism, and just stating a view, like painting a picture. Some might feel irritated, thinking Spinoza's picture is more like Hegel's than Hegel allows. Perhaps Hegel sees substance as inactive, and Spinoza intends a different picture. But the point here is only what Spinoza's reasons would show. A Spinoza without reason Hegel would see no need to take so seriously as to require immanent critique.

There is no space here to try to canvass *all* texts to argue that there is no passage in which Hegel suggests an insubstantial critique or a question-begging argument. But this is remote from my focus. I am not trying to evaluate the goodness of two people, or keep score by counting mistakes, or raise or lower the status of either person. I follow the spirit of Hegel's engagement with Spinoza: focus most on finding the strongest reasons, strong enough for their engagement to be of most philosophical interest.

I begin with the case that Spinoza's use of the PSR forces elimination of determinacy (§2.1). What is more distinctively Hegelian, and more distinctive to my reading, will be the way this PSR attack combines with a second, without need of the PSR: *from* substance as purely affirmative or involving no negation (forced by an appeal to an immediacy reason) *to* at least the elimination of the finite (§2.2, and the combination in §2.3).

§2.1 The *Nihilo* Abyss of Mediation

Hegel's abyss critique alleges that Spinoza's substance must be indeterminate. One way of making the point is this:

> ... in the Spinozistic system everything is only thrown into this abyss, but nothing comes out of it (*es kommt nichts heraus*), and the particular of which he speaks is taken up from representation (*Vorstellung*) without being justified; if it were justified, Spinoza would have to deduce it, derive it from his substance.[45]

---

[44] There is also no space here for consideration of determinacy in the form of infinite modes.
[45] GW 30,3: 1278, cf. VGP 3:288/20:166.

A reference in the *Logic* to "Spinoza's *substance*" and the "abyss" is similarly followed by:

> With Spinoza the difference, the attributes, thought and extension, and then also the modes, the affections, and all other determinations, comes quite empirically. (SL 21:381)

This much seems clearly alleged: Spinoza "speaks" of determinacy (modes and attributes), and *does not intend to eliminate it*; but to be *entitled* to this he would have to derive it (rather than assuming it or taking it as established empirically), *and this he cannot do*.

I argue Hegel has strong reasons for concluding that: Spinoza's own reasons for monism *both* require that determinacy be entirely eliminated if no derivation showing what it "comes out of" can be given, and *also* prevent such derivation (*in a sense of derivation to which Spinoza's own reasoning should commit him*).

2.1.1 The Nihilo *Abyss for Finite Modes*

Here is an outline of the case that Spinoza must eliminate finite modes because he would have to, and cannot, derive them from substance. I begin with three premises I think clearly internal to Spinoza's monism:

S1: Everything that exists has a cause of its existence.[46]
S2: The only cause for the existence of anything is God.[47]
S3: Everything that exists is caused by God. (from S1 and S2, but also independently stated and used by Spinoza)

We can then try to argue that (4) is internal to Spinoza, forcing (C):

4: God cannot be the cause of the existence of the finite.
C: Thus, the finite does not exist. (From S3 and 4)

S1 is internal to Spinoza. The critique need *not* assume the more extreme idea that Spinoza appeals to a broad fact-PSR, nor the idea that any PSR is the single common thread in the argument, nor even just at work throughout the whole. The critique can rest on Spinoza's clearly stating and using Bi-PSR in E1P11D2 and so in the shortly following case for monism: the existence side of it is S1.[48]

---

[46] I leave out "or reason"; it could not matter given S3 is internal.
[47] As we will see, cause by mode would also be cause by God: by God *as modified by a modification*.
[48] I believe E1 refers back to E1P11 for support 10 times.

S2 also seems important to monism: there is nothing else to serve as cause or reason but God.[49]

Even if S1 and S2 were not present, and/or did not support S3, we could just start with S3; it seems core to Spinoza's monism, and is often stated, e.g.: "God is the ... cause of all things."[50] We will soon see that Spinoza argues from this in E1P28D.

Also internal to Spinoza is the basic logic of using such considerations to *eliminate* things. Having stated the Bi-PSR in E1P11D2, he argues that there could be no cause of "any other substance but God" (E1P14D), and so he eliminates other substances. Contingency (in some sense that would need further interpretation) could not be caused by God, and so is eliminated (E1P29D).

So finite modes must be eliminated if they cannot be caused by God. Even defenses of Spinoza should concede this much, and often do; I will note some below.[51]

To deal with Hegel's texts it is helpful to state the argument as well in terms of the *nihilo* PSR. Hegel often uses the Latin, but sometimes translates into German: "aus Nichts wird Nichts" (nothing comes from nothing). So here is a parallel to the above:

> S1*: Nothing comes from nothing.
> S2*: God is the only thing for anything to come from.
> S3*: There is nothing that does not come from God. (S1*, S2*)
> 4*: The finite cannot come from God.
> C*: The finite is nothing. (S3*, 4*)

Hegel often expresses versions of 4* in criticisms of Spinoza, e.g.

> ... modes are also determinations ... they do not come from the substance (*aus der Substanz kommen sie nicht*) ... (GW 23,1:371).

With respect to the "finiteness," "how that comes out (*herauskommt*) of substance is not grasped."[52] With respect to God: "everything goes only in, not out (*nicht heraus*)."[53] Hegel also associates the *nihilo* PSR with the Parmenides of Elea and the view that there is only *indeterminate* being, sometimes mentioning Spinoza[54] – and that those who hold the principle may not be aware that it forces indeterminacy.[55]

---

[49] Stein gets to my S3 via this S2 at (2021: 277).
[50] E1P18 (I return to the immanent causality mentioned here; see also 16, 24C, 26, 28D, etc.
[51] E.g. Garrett 2012: 254.   [52] (VL 113/GW 23,2:737)
[53] (VGP 20:173/3:264), cf. "nichts heraus" (23,1:376). The context is the attributes, but the passage refers to "everything."
[54] E.g. Mich. 188.
[55] SL 21:71. This last passage is ambiguous, so I do not rest on it. About the connection between Spinoza and Parmenides, see §2.2.1 and §3.1.

Philosophical defense: We can best defend the force of the critique as immanent by looking to *Ethics* 1, P28. Spinoza argues by raising a problem about the cause of *any one particular* finite mode. Spinoza himself denies that God – *from the absolute nature of God/an attribute of God, as opposed to God as affected by a mode* – could be the cause: "whatever follows from the absolute nature of one of God's attributes is infinite and eternal" (E1P28D, repeating E1P21). Similarly, God as modified by an infinite mode – whatever exactly that is – cannot cause something finite (E1P28D, citing E1P22). So the commitment is something like: whatever is caused by or comes from something infinite, *as infinite* – rather than affected by a finite mode – must be infinite (call this ∞ commitment or ∞C).

While not necessary here, for those seeking a deeper internal root of ∞C, Spinoza argues for it in the early *Short Treatise* on grounds of . . . the *nihilo* PSR; some interpreters see the *Ethics* in this light as well.[56]

For any particular finite mode, E1P28 solves the problem of its cause by *exhaustive elimination*: The absolute nature of the one substance cannot be the cause. And "nothing exists but substance and its modes." *Thus* the cause of any particular finite mode must be another finite mode. This does not violate S3, requiring that God causes everything: the cause *is* God, "insofar as it was modified by a modification which is finite" (E1P28D). Since the point reapplies to the causing mode, Spinoza gets a desired conclusion: these finite causes in substance extend "*ad infinitum*" (E1P28D).

But the question Hegel raises is not about the cause of the existence of a particular finite mode; it is about the existence of the finite modes at all. Consider "finite reality" in this critique of Spinoza:

> The world has no true reality, and all this that we know as the world has been cast into the abyss of the one identity. There is therefore no such thing as finite reality . . .[57]

And here *Spinoza's own* exhaustive elimination of causes in E1P28 supports the elimination of *all* options for a cause:

The absolute nature of God/an attribute of God cannot be the cause. Nor God as affected by an infinite mode. Whatever is caused by any of this must be infinite, by Spinoza's own reasoning in E1P28D (∞C).

And Spinoza has argued that the only other option would be a finite mode. But a finite mode cannot cause the existence of the finite modes, or it would cause its own existence; modes are clearly defined as merely contingent on substance.

---

[56] CW 66; Della Rocca (2008: 71f.); Primus (2023: 23).
[57] Some might seek escape by denying there is such thing as *the finite modes as a whole*, but Spinoza cannot (E2P13SL7s). Also (E1P5D) asks us to collect together and set aside *all* affections.

So: considerations internal to Spinoza force the conclusion that God cannot be the cause of the finite (4/4*) and indeed that Spinoza cannot provide *any* cause, and so (C/C*) the denial of the existence of the finite.[58]

Objections and replies: Neither the Hegel criticism noted here, nor my defense, depends in any way on foisting on Spinoza any uncharitable reading of the geometric method as weak: the key is rather Spinoza's stating the Bi-PSR, and using it; and Spinoza's reasoning in E1P28D.[59]

Some seem to think to rebut Hegel's critique by citing text in Spinoza affirming modes and other forms of determinacy, or making commitments that require this affirmation.[60] This is zero rebuttal to the abyss critique on which we are focusing;[61] on the contrary, it is *part* of the critique: Spinoza's reasons for eliminating other substances force a conception of substance *contrary* to his intent, first of all, one without any finitude in it.

Some seem to think Hegel's criticisms fail because of uncharitable assumptions about Spinoza's intent concerning substance: for example, that Spinoza intends it to be somehow "immobile," "rigid," "inert," lacking "movement" or "life."[62] But the intent is not the point, again, and this critique and my defense required none of this, only Spinoza's own way of treating substance in thinking about causes.

Some argue that Hegel here begs the question by assuming Spinoza must "derive" finite modes either in some special distinctively Hegelian sense foreign to Spinoza, derivation by some kind of dialectical negation.[63] That would be weak. But we have just seen that Hegel's critique requires only a demand that Spinoza derive the finite *in the sense that Spinoza's own arguments insist on derivation via causes, in the Bi-PSR of E1P11D2, and in the case of a finite mode in E1P28.*

Some argue that Hegel fails by overlooking Spinoza's view of God as *immanent* cause of the finite, perhaps because this leaves no need for finitude to come out of God if it is always already there.[64]

On the one hand, if Spinoza allows God as immanent cause of something finite, he is presumably aware of it; but he *still denies in E1P28 that the absolute nature of God can cause the existence of a finite mode*. Spinoza's own E1P28 argument would fail if he allowed: 'all we need say about this is that a finite

---

[58] Some other old recognition of the problem: Caird 1888: 142; Leibniz 1989: 238.
[59] Macherey (2011, Ch. 2) defends Spinoza by attacking uncharitable reading of that method.
[60] E.g. Bartuschat 2007 on Spinoza's focus on an individual's path to wisdom; On Melamed (2010), see §2.3.
[61] Acknowledged by E.g. (Parkinson 1977: 456); (Yovel 1992: 33); (Newlands 2011: 102); (Hübner 2015: 227).
[62] E.g. Macherey 2011: 14, 27, 30, 31.   [63] E.g. Melamed 2010: 82–83.
[64] Bartuschat 2007: 113; Sandkaulen 2019: 328.

mode is always already in God'. He is more demanding. I defended Hegel by simply using Spinoza's reasoning here against him.

On the other hand, say *any* version of this defense worked: imagine Spinoza allowed a special kind of X-causation, in which substance *can* be the special X-cause of the finite. Not only is E1P28 lost, for reasons above, but the case for monism seems to me gravely wounded: Anti-monists can rejoice. For they can *with equal right* propose a special Z-causality *by which God can Z-cause the existence of distinct substances, creating the world out of nothing*. This would escape the force of Spinoza's case for monism from the start of E1P1-6*'s* denial of this possibility. The case for eliminating multiple substances draws its strength from being more principled; that very strength threatens to eliminate finitude as well.

Some Spinoza interpreters cede the internal issue, and see it solved by Spinoza with some kind of causal mediator(s) between God, as infinite, and the finite.[65] But any anti-dualist, like Hegel, would *welcome* this attempt, as clarifying the force of the problem. Compare: those worried about Descartes on interaction will see appeals to a mediator between thinking and extended substances as highlighting the difficulty, not solving it. Does the mediator count for the purposes of the ∞C as infinite, or finite? Either way, the problem of the lack of a cause persists on one side or the other.

Some cede the problem and try to solve it by appeal to what Spinoza calls "the whole of nature," "one individual, whose parts, that is, all bodies, vary in infinite ways" (E2P13SL7s). Perhaps this "infinite individual," *as infinite*, could be caused by the absolute nature of God; and perhaps it would not then need to cause the finite modes, as it would already have them as "parts."[66]

I think Spinoza's commitments should block this. God is not divisible (E1P13), and no substance, as infinite, could be (E1P13S). Spinoza considers the possibility of having finite parts, saying this would leave substance dependent, rather than having existence in its nature.[67] The threat persists as concern that something with finite parts would not be infinite, in anything like God's sense, and ∞C should block God causing it.[68]

I conclude that Hegel identifies genuinely internal reasons, having to do with dependence or mediation and the *nihilo* PSR, threatening to force the wholesale elimination of the finite. I will return in §2.3 to the way in which further seeming escapes from this argument would be foreclosed by the way it combines with the argument of §2.2.

---

[65] E.g. Wolfson 1934: 390.   [66] E.g. Garrett 2018, ch. 4.
[67] E1P13CS seems to rule it absurd that substance *could have parts*.
[68] As (Primus 2023) argues at length, recognizing a kind of acosmism.

2.1.2 A Nihilo Abyss for Distinct Attributes?

As I said above, I think losing the finite is enough of a conflict within Spinoza's philosophy for an immanent critique. But let me say something more brief about Hegel's worry that Spinoza's reasons force elimination of distinct attributes as well.

Spinoza's attributes are obviously not meant to be distinct from one another, nor from God, in the sense of being separate substances. They seem meant to be distinct from one another at very least in the sense that one can be conceived without any other (E1P10). But, after this, Spinoza scholarship reflects wide-ranging debate about even the most basic issues about attributes – too much to allow full defense of Hegel's critique on this score.

But consider Hegel's charge in passages like this:

> ... everything goes only in, not out (*nicht heraus*). The determinations are not developed from substance, it does not resolve itself into these attributes.[69]

Many see Hegel's worry as sunk by a misunderstanding: they say substance is not supposed to be prior to its attributes, so that some derivation for the latter from the former could be required; it is rather more that the attributes "*are* substance."[70]

And it is certainly true that Spinoza treats substance and attributes as so intimately close that we can draw inferences about attributes directly from features of substance: e.g. attributes are conceived through themselves because substance is conceived through itself (E1P10D).

But this does not block a *nihilo* abyss critique. There is a more general question: What is the reason for or cause of the distinctness of distinct attributes? Hegel, we will see, also auditions other possible answers, aside from substance (§2.1.3), and so does not seem to see the worry as predicated on taking substance as prior to attribute and the only possible answer.

Perhaps the point of the just-mentioned rejoinders to Hegel is that the very question is a mistake, and so without need of an answer, *specifically because attributes just are substance*. To me this strengthens Hegel's worry. Say we go all in on *attributes are substance*; but substance is one and not many; it threatens to follow that attributes are one, eliminating distinctions between them, and so eliminating determinacy in this form.

But perhaps the answer to that concern is that there is some explanation of why attributes should rather be many? Fine. But this seems to recognize the legitimacy of the Hegelian question of the reasons for there being many.

---

[69] (VGP 20:173/3:264), cf. "nichts heraus" (23,1:376). The context is the attributes, but the passage refers to "everything."
[70] Garrett 2012: 258. For similar rejections of Hegel: Gueroult 1968: 429; Macherey 2011: 108.

And so it seems to me not so uncharitable to consider the possibility that the question can arise for Spinoza. Here is how I would argue there is some internal pressure to allow it both to arise, and to need answering. Consider Spinoza's argument, followed above, requiring that "[t]wo or more distinct things (*res*) are distinguished from one another" by something, either modes or attributes (E1P4). Being consistent or non-*ad hoc* seems to me some reason for Spinoza to need some cause of or reason for the distinctness of distinct attributes.

Granted, *perhaps* E1P4 itself is not *intended* to apply to attributes. E.g. perhaps "things" (*res*) excludes attributes? But the concern is not insubstantial, as if it were about a word choice; it is about reasons for monism. Including substance but excepting attributes from what otherwise seemed a general principle – namely, that distinction depends on distinguishers – would understandably look to the anti-monist *ad hoc*, tailored to the desired conclusion of one substance with many attributes. Anti-monists will rejoice that they could, seemingly with equal right, propose an exception by which distinct *substances* also do not require any distinguishers. That would reject E1P4 – erasing any reason for monism going through the beginning of the *Ethics*.

To me it seems then not uncharitable to try to *defend* Spinoza as more principled, even if that means allowing the question to arise, and to require an answer: what would distinguish distinct attributes? E1P4 allows either modes or attributes. E1P5 rules out modes as distinguishers; Hegel cites this (§1.1.3) and we will shortly see him use it to try to push the attributes into the abyss (§2.1.3). What seems left by Spinoza's exhaustiveness claim is for *attributes* to distinguish themselves from one another. I think Spinoza could not say this. For that answer seems to require that it would be part of what one attribute is for it *not* to be the others. That seems to conflict with the attributes being conceived through themselves (E1P10) and involving no negation (E1D6E).[71] Compare finite modes: Spinoza says that being finite involves there being something conceivably greater; he *agrees* that this means finitude involves negation in this way, as Hegel is aware (§2.2.1). (Note: Hegel is often seen as merely assuming that attributes must involve negation; that would be weak, but there is no need for it: the point here is to charitably *allow* Spinoza these attempts to avoid the abyss, and to point out that this one fails because *the attempted defense of Spinoza itself* would see attributes as involving negation; see below §2.2.2.)

So, there is at least some reason to think that the distinctness of attributes would have to come from somewhere, or else be eliminated, and that it can come neither from modes nor attributes. To me, someone pursuing this would be

---

[71] Note: No *assumption* that attributes must involve negation to be determinate; here he takes this as encouraged by genuinely immanent engagement.

charitable to at least allow the question: could Spinoza be saved by consideration of whether the distinctness of attributes could "come out of" or be explained by substance, in some other sense? The critics of Hegel who think that question cannot even arise seem to me to assume and agree with Hegel's answer: substance cannot be the reason for this attribute not being that attribute. For example, given the attributes involve no negation, and the intimate connection to substance, substance too is purely affirmative.

I make no attempt to canvass all passages and rule out Hegel having a mistaken interpretation somewhere of the substance-attribute relation. But my focus is the abyss critique. Although there is no space for full defense, I have argued in this section that these worries, at least, need not affect it. However, we have not noted all of the possible answers allowed by Hegel to the Spinozist defense of attributes.

2.1.3 Ideality and Acosmism: No Rebuttal to the Abyss Critique

Hegel considers and argues against another way to defend Spinoza: perhaps Spinoza *himself* advocates a downgrade in the ontological status of the attributes and/or modes, and this evades the problem. In particular, perhaps if attributes and/or modes were downgraded to a merely ideal or mind-dependent ontological status, then the answer to the challenge would be clear: they would not be objects whose mind-independent existence or real existence in substance would need to depend on substance or similar; they would depend on the mind, being something like appearances in this sense.

My sense is that the literature on this tends to portray Hegel's critique as failing due to an incorrect idealist interpretation of Spinoza.[72] But we have already seen above how the abyss critique attacks both modes and attributes, *without need of any such interpretation*. There is nothing uncharitable about allowing and considering another possible defense, via idealism. And so it is worth Hegel's showing that this downgrade in ontological status could not succeed at avoiding total elimination.

Consider again Spinoza's definition of attribute:

> By attribute I mean that which the intellect perceives of substance as constituting its essence. (E1D4)

Let us consider the definition in light of Hegel's *nihilo* critique, which would ask on what the distinctness of the attributes depends. In this light, it is charitable to allow both possibilities: *either* the definition does not make the attributes depend on "the intellect," *or* it does.

---

[72] E.g. Melamed 2010: 81; Macherey 2011: 84.

If it does not, then no such mind-dependence can help avoid the *nihilo* critique in the previous section, which is then complete: the distinctness of the attributes must come from something, and it cannot come from modes, attributes, or substance; so, it must be eliminated.

It is charitable to Spinoza to consider the possibility that attributes *are* meant to depend on "the intellect," and that this might resolve the threat.

But Hegel sees and states precisely why this cannot help Spinoza. In the first instance, it would make the nature of the attributes depend on a mode, which violates their priority. Hegel says:

> ... the *understanding* [*Verstand*, intellect] is assumed to be by nature posterior to the attribute (for Spinoza defines it as *mode*) ... (SL 11:377)

Spinoza does seem to take the "intellect" as a mode:

> By intellect [*intellectum*] (as is self-evident) we do not understand absolute thought, but only a definite mode of thinking ... (E1P31D).

And Hegel is entirely correct that Spinoza takes modes as posterior, and nothing that could ground distinctness of the attributes, which are prior (Cf. E1P5D; §1.1.3).

Perhaps this is too quick. Perhaps attributes depend not on any finite mind, as a mode, but rather on the *attribute* of thought (perhaps what Spinoza means by "absolute thought" in the last passage). I see this again as reinforcing Hegel's critique: what we had taken for other attributes would all *depend* on the attribute of thought; but for them to be many would now seem again to require negation in the attribute of thought; alternatively, since to be an attribute is to be explanatorily basic, there would be pressure to rule thought the only attribute – and that would eliminate determinate distinctions between attributes.[73]

In sum, Hegel shows that no such ontological *downgrade* of attributes to ideal status could escape the case that this determinacy must be entirely eliminated, contra Spinoza's intent.

This topic connects to the claim of Hegel – and many at the time – that Spinoza, contrary to his reputation as an atheist, is an "acosmist."[74] But this has many meanings in Hegel's context. Sometimes "acosmism" is used to mean that only God is *fully* real, and the finite *downgraded to less so*. Elsewhere it means *entirely eliminating* the world. Where someone uses "acosmism" in the former sense, they might be an idealist endorsing it in their own name, or reading it as Spinoza's *intent* and supporting this. Where used in the latter sense this tends to be a *critique* asserting that Spinoza fails relative to his intent to avoid wholesale

---

[73] On this line in British idealist interpreters of Spinoza, Newlands 2011: 112.
[74] For discussion and many references in Hegel and others, Melamed (2010), to which I return in §2.3.

elimination. In this second sense, my topic could be called the "acosmism critique." But the ambiguity in "acosmism" has allowed Spinoza's defenders to portray a rejoinder to the former line of thought – to an acosmism *interpretation of Spinoza's intent* – namely, as downgrading the finite – as if it could be any rejoinder to the latter *critique* – to the critique that Spinoza must entirely eliminate determinacy. But to argue that Spinoza does not intend the downgrade in status of the finite does not block any of my defense of Hegel's critique here: the critique is all the easier if the defense via downgrade need not be considered. To be clear here, then, I favor the term "abyss critique."

§2.2 The Abyss of Pure Affirmation, or Immediacy Abyss

An objection to the *nihilo* abyss argument above would be that it gives too much weight, in Spinoza, to the PSR. But we are really getting into very distinctively Hegelian territory when we combine this with an independent line of argument in Hegel that Spinoza must eliminate determinacy, stemming not from the PSR but from Spinoza's own commitments about God as affirmative, involving no negation. So I add to the '*nihilo* abyss' what I call an 'abyss of pure affirmation'.

Further, to whatever degree a Spinozist takes weight off mediation in the form of the PSR and transfers it to a claim to find reason in a supposedly immediate grasp of the existence of God or the one substance, we have seen reason to think this requires the affirmative conception of God – otherwise, immediacy cannot resolve the worry about an internal contradiction in the conception of God (§1.2). So defending against the above by taking weight off of the PSR and considerations of mediation will tend to put more weight on immediacy, and inflame the other strand of critique, which we could also call an 'immediacy abyss'.

Later we will find in the *Logic* the ultimate abyss for immediacy more generally: Hegel will argue that the appeal to immediacy as a reason, in our supposed grasp of something, could not be distinguished from our sense of what that thing is: it would not stand in mediation relations with anything else, nor would it have distinct parts within it standing in such relations; the distinction between grasp and *in itself* collapses, and everything here ends up indeterminate (§3.2). But in this section I pursue, in part as preparation, a form of argument more focused on the specifics in Spinoza: the modes, attributes, and so on.

2.2.1 An Affirmation or Immediacy Abyss for Finite Modes

I defend in this section just one prong of the 'affirmation abyss' attack: the case that Spinoza's affirmative conception of God requires the elimination of the finite modes. I will defend my own position on this, namely, that this attack draws its real force from the larger idea I am defending here, about its combination with the *nihilo* abyss, above, and the distinction between mediation and immediacy. But we can start with an article by Hübner articulating the basic case about affirmation in its own terms. Quoting from Hübner's premises:

> **S1.** " ... being or reality ... as it is in itself is positive" or involves no negation.
> **S2.** " ... finite things are constituted in part by negation ... ."[75]
> **C.** Being or reality as it is in itself includes no finite things.

S2 seems expressed by and internal to Spinoza: " ... in fact to be finite is in part a negation and to be infinite is the unqualified affirmation of the existence of some nature" (E1P8S1). If more is needed, then I think it is generally acknowledged that reference to *limitation* in Spinoza's account of the finite is also a reference to negation:

> A thing is said to be finite in its own kind when it can be limited by another thing of the same nature. For example, a body is said to be finite because we can always conceive of another body greater than it. (E1D2)

Its being finite involves it *not* being something greater.

Spinoza seems to hold S1. In the *Ethics,* reality includes only one substance, God. Further,

> By God I mean an absolutely infinite being, that is, substance consisting of infinite attributes, each of which expresses eternal and infinite essence. (E1D6)

To clarify, Spinoza adds:

> ... if a thing is absolutely infinite, whatever expresses essence and does not involve any negation belongs to its essence. (E1D6E)[76]

In sum, there is only God, and God's nature or essence involves no negation.

With respect to S2, above, Hegel is aware that Spinoza thinks the finite involves negation. For example, in discussing Spinoza: "That, in virtue of which a single thing is, is negation."[77] "The negative" is taken by Spinoza "to be the determinateness of finite things."[78] And Hegel states in this way the threat of affirmation abyss: modifications[79] are not present in being or reality in itself or in truth:

> The world has no true reality, but all this is thrown into the abyss of the one identity. There is therefore nothing in finite reality: this has no truth; according to Spinoza, what 'is' is 'God' alone.[80]

---

[75] Hübner 2015: 222.   [76] Hübner 2015: 224.
[77] VGP25/6 104. Translated differently in Brown 154.   [78] GW 15:10. Cf. §2.2.2.
[79] Hegel should say *finite* modifications; he pays the infinite modes little heed.
[80] Mich 891, cf. VGP 3:281/30,3:1282/20:195.

And:

> ... God alone is the positive, the affirmative, and consequently the one substance; all other things, on the contrary, are only modifications of this substance, and are nothing in and for themselves. (VGP 3:236/Mich. 893)

Now I want to take a step back from Hübner's outline, plugging this into my idea here, about the two-part mediation/immediacy structure; so, first: Say we relieve the PSR pressure towards the *nihilo* abyss, above, by shifting the weight to a claim to find reason in an immediate grasp of God as existing. We then face pressure towards this affirmative conception of God as containing no negation, a reason Spinoza not only does but must hold this. We could also call this also an *immediacy abyss*, even though the threat arises anyway so long as Spinoza treats God as purely affirmative (thus my main term, 'abyss of affirmation').

Second, I can grant here a sense in which the affirmation-abyss criticism *on its own* can seem weak: Hegel's passages draw the inference that seems to follow, namely, that finite things have "no true reality," and are "nothing in and for themselves." But perhaps this should be obvious, intended by Spinoza as a mere *downgrade* to their ontological status to not being "in and for themselves", rather than *wholesale elimination?*

I would defend the worry by asking: given the purely positive, infinite God, what sense can we make of some non-eliminated but downgraded or not in-itself status for the modes? The answer can seem obvious: the modes *derive* from God, and in this sense have no place in reality *in itself*, while not being totally eliminated; their status is that of a merely dependent rather than in-itself reality.[81] But the context in my treatment shows the problem with this: it drives us right back into the teeth of the *nihilo* abyss defended above (§2.1), in arguing that Spinoza cannot account for any derivation of the finite from God.[82]

Perhaps there are other ways of making sense of a downgraded-but-not-eliminated status of modes? For example, say we try this: the modes are *part* of God, and in this sense not any aspect of being or reality *in itself* simply because too partial, as it were. But God, again, as infinite substance, cannot have parts; it would merely depend on them (E1P13). Hübner says, for Spinoza, "To think of being as differentiated through negation into finite particulars is an error analogous to thinking that substance has 'really distinct' parts" (223).

---

[81] Newlands 2011 finds what I call the affirmation abyss weak, I think for this reason, and seeks strength in the PSR issue. I think strength requires keeping the affirmation abyss in play (§2.3).

[82] Again, the problem draws *only* on the sense of derivation to which Spinoza's argumentation and his PSR commit him.

Another possibility, considered by Hegel and Hübner, is that modes are not any aspect of anything in itself, but still have some status – and escape total elimination – insofar as they are *for us*. Certainly Hegel at least considers this, referring to "mere modifications which only exist for us apart from God" (VGP 3:270/ Mich. 882). Hübner argues that there are texts in Spinoza which might help such a reading of Spinoza's intent. But whether or not this "for us" status is intended by Spinoza, and whether or not Hegel thinks it is, or just considers it – I don't see reason any of that would blunt the force of the affirmation abyss critique. For we saw Hegel's clear and precise point above about mind-dependence failing to save the attributes from total elimination (§2.1.3). And that point applies just as well to show that this cannot save the modes: modes are not only not prior to attributes, they are also not prior to themselves. We cannot parry the threat of total elimination of the finite by saying it exists but merely as for *finite* minds – that, as Hübner puts it, begs the question about the existence of the finite.[83]

I will add only one point here, about Hegel's association of Spinoza with Parmenides when discussing Spinoza in the context of immediacy.[84] Hegel takes Parmenides to hold that there is only being, itself purely affirmative, involving no negation; and to take being as entirely indeterminate in the sense that there are neither determinate differences within it, nor is there anything else from which it differs, or any determinate time at which it could have come to be, and so on. Interpreters often think to defend Spinoza against Hegel by pointing out that Spinoza is not a Parmenidean, in the sense that much that he writes is incompatible with this view.[85] But once again this point about his intent is not a rejoinder to Hegel, but part of Hegel's critique about an internal tension. The affirmative abyss discussed here then also amounts to the idea that Spinoza, in treating God as involving no negation, raises the danger of getting pulled along in Parmenides' case against determinacy.

In sum, I have defended a second strand of Hegel's abyss critique, from Spinoza's view of God as purely affirmative: an affirmation abyss. With this we can begin to see that the real force of the overall abyss critique lies in the combination: For perhaps the *nihilo* abyss critique can be parried by shifting the weight of monism onto immediacy; but this requires the view of God as purely affirmative, and inflames the problem of the affirmation abyss. The latter can also be parried, for example by seeing it as only downgrading the status of the finite to merely derivative; but this will inflame the former critique.

---

[83] Hübner 2015: 235. She takes seriously the idea that a finite thing might have a purely positive essence in striving to persist in being (cf. Macherey 2011: 172; Lin 2019: 131). But I think *finitude* is lost without just the reference to negation Spinoza makes – as less than either God/ infinity or a greater finite.
[84] Starting SL 21:71. [85] E.g. Macherey 2011: 86, 91; Sandkaulen 2019: 326–28.

2.2.2 All Determination is Negation? No Threat to Hegel's Abyss Critique

Interpreters often defend Spinoza by claiming that Hegel's critique is question-begging in (supposedly) assuming a principle that Spinoza would reject, namely, *all determination is negation, omnis determinatio est negatio* (I call this the '*omnis* principle').[86]

I agree that Spinoza would reject the "all" (*omnis*) part of this: he takes negation as constitutive of the finite, *but not the attributes / God*. I have no objection to critics arguing that Spinoza never included the "all" (*omnis*).[87]

But the first thing I want to say about this issue is that *none of the arguments above assume any such principle:* Spinoza states and uses the PSR, and I have defended a case from *his own principle* to the elimination of finite modes, and more briefly given reason to worry it threatens determinate differences between attributes as well (§2.1). Meanwhile, in the case of the finite modes, they again seem threatened by Spinoza's affirmative conception of God, where there is reason to think that an appeal to an immediacy reason would require that conception (§2.2.1). Again: *none of that requires the omnis principle*. So, whatever Hegel's view of Spinoza's view about the *omnis* principle, I don't see how this could encourage any worry about the combination of all of the above strands of abyss critique. (I will come back to the case in the *Logic* for the radical indeterminacy (ruling out anything like modes *or attributes*) for any object of such immediacy (§3.1).

There is a lot Hegel could try to *show* and in this way *say* about the *omnis* without necessarily begging the question. There would be nothing question-begging about Hegel trying to develop, *through genuinely immanent critique*, his own final position, *different* from Spinoza's. While there will be neither space nor need here for complete defense, I will argue below (§3) that Hegel sees the *Logic,* through immanent critique of the metaphysics of immediacy and mediation, as *deriving* the position that *all* determinacy is negation.

Further, there would then be nothing question-begging about Hegel trying to retrospectively *explain* in these terms why Spinoza fell into the abyss: it can be independently shown that he suffers from internal conflicts, but he might have avoided them, we see much later, had he seen that *all* determination is negation. Consider this:

> ... negativity ... If it is taken only to be the determinateness of finite things (*omnis determinatio est negatio*) then we are already thinking of it outside of absolute substance and have allowed finite things to fall outside of it ...[88]

---
[86] Parkinson 1977: 454; Bartuschat 2007: 111; Melamed 2012a: 187–88.
[87] Bartuschat 2007; Melamed 2010. [88] GW 15:10/Heid 8–9.

Hegel is under no illusion that Spinoza would apply the principle to God; this is a *criticism:* Spinoza does *not* apply the principle to everything, and leaves God purely affirmative; for immanent critique all that is needed is that a purely affirmative God, Hegel argues (without assuming *omnis*, as far as I can see) brings abyss troubles.

And while there is no space for defense here, there would then be nothing question-begging about *trying* to argue that Spinoza *should* have seen that all determinacy is negation. Perhaps because he thinks mediation and immediacy through so far that he *should* have seen the abyss, and through this that all determinacy must rather be negation.

Granted, Hegel does call the *omnis* "Spinoza's proposition," and seems to think Spinoza wrote down the words "*omnis determinatio est negatio*" (SL 21:101). So it is possible for all I argue that Hegel sometimes argues that one internal problem for Spinoza is that he wrote the word "*omnis*" (or Hegel thinks he did). Even if true, this would be a shockingly insubstantial critique: from this alone it would only follow that Spinoza could and should cross out that one word! I think it is clear that Hegel thinks Spinoza's position faces substantial immanent threat, from which there is something important philosophically to be learned. And my focus has been to argue that Hegel does identify such threats (§2.1–2), and to defend them, without reliance on any assumption about the *omnis*.

§2.3 Bringing it Together

In general, my argument suggests that, if you focus on only one form of Hegel's challenge – concerning just mediation or immediacy – there will appear to be a way to meet it. But such a strategy will tend to rest more weight on the other form of reason, and so tend to inflame the other challenge that is held out of view.

Let us consider again in this light a new objection to Hegel's case that Spinoza's PSR forces elimination of distinct attributes: The Bi-PSR says: "[f]or each thing there must be assigned a cause, *or* reason (*causa seu ratio*), both for its existence and for its nonexistence" (E1P11D2). God is defined as a substance with infinite attributes, and there cannot be any reason or cause of the non-existence of God: whatever served as the cause would have to share an attribute with God, and Spinoza argues against attribute sharing. And that is the reason, as it were, why there is a substance with infinite attributes – staving off the threat of their elimination.

And perhaps a similar objection could argue that there can be no reason against God as modified in infinite ways by finite modes, finding this reason for the existence of finite modes.

Spinoza includes this way of reasoning in some of his cases for the existence of God (E1P11D2). Some worry that such an argument for God's existence turns on an assumed "bias" towards existence or reality (Lin 2019: 65). Whether that is right or not, I do think this problem is a threat to the defenses of Spinoza above: it appears that such a defender just presumes the determinacy of substance, absent reason *against*, refusing to consider the other side of this, namely, the possibility that this might fail to obtain due to lack of reason *for* it. Perhaps to some this seems like a standoff, with each side biased in one direction. But think of Hegel's charge as alleging that Spinoza's reasons for monism, if supporting monism, would force elimination of determinacy. Part of the point is that Spinoza's strength of reasons lies in his being principled, rather than *ad hoc*. To say this is a standoff would be to admit to an arbitrariness on this point; the anti-monist could then rejoice and introduce arbitrary distinctions to save a multiplicity of substances. So to me this seems more like accepting Hegel's charge that, to whatever degree Spinoza has non-arbitrary reasons for monism, they would force the abyss.

Perhaps Spinoza can respond rather by offering further reason here. He argues that "[t]he more reality or being a thing has, the more attributes it has" (E1P9). (And perhaps a similar case could be made for an infinity of finite modifications of substance.[89]) One worry would be that the case here again turns on the above bias (Lin 2019: 71). But setting that aside, for this to answer the charge, I think the situation would have to be this: *prior* to the operation of a PSR, which might threaten the attributes, we already have access to the existence of a God with infinite reality or being; having that, we can safely introduce the PSR, and plug this God into the PSR, providing affirmative reason for the multiplicity of attributes. But then what would provide the initial reason for a God of infinite reality, independent of the PSR? I think the real contender in Spinoza is a claim to an immediate grasp of the existence of such a God. But we have seen reason to think this itself would force elimination – at least of the modes, with more complete indeterminacy to be discussed below (§3) – prior to the entry of the PSR. To so combine immediacy and mediation in defense of Spinoza cannot escape the combination of Hegelian attacks.

With respect to the combination attack, it is also worth looking briefly at perhaps the most fully developed defense of Spinoza: Melamed seems to, and is widely taken to, deny that Hegel meets his own standard of internal critique: "Hegel failed to meet Spinoza on the latter's ground." Hegel is supposed to need his own external assumption about the need for a derivation of modes via dialectical negation. Melamed's view is that modes are rather "the properties (*proprietates*) that follow from the definition of the thing defined." So, "Hegel's complaint about the lack of derivation of modes is unjustified" (2010: 82–83).

---

[89] I think this is Garrett's defense here: "A substance that is variegated into infinitely many finite quasi-substantial modes expresses more reality and perfection" (2012: 254).

But given the distinction between strands of critique above, consider what follows *if* this is a promising approach to the affirmation abyss (§2.2) – seeking a non-eliminated status for modes in a purely affirmative God. *It still cedes the immanent force of the nihilo abyss* (§2.2–3)! For whatever Spinoza's position on definitions is, it does not affect the concern about divine causality in the *nihilo* abyss. For he is aware of his position on this, and still gives the argument by *exhaustive elimination* in E1P28: he does not allow or even consider whether a finite mode could derive from God in this definitional or "*proprietates*" sense. But I won't argue this point: Melamed himself concedes that his idea is *no* defense to the PSR concern, but rather raises again its question about why modes exist: "[o]ne can further press Spinoza by asking *why* the modes follow from God's essence"; this "turns out to be particularly disturbing for Spinoza" (83n31).

Elsewhere Melamed recognizes that this is a worry of *Hegel's*, and is *strong*: about Spinoza's "substance-mode bifurcation,"

> ... one may invoke the PSR in order to obliterate it ... denying the reality of ... modes ... One can now see why Hegel claims that '*ex nihilo nihil fit*,' a variant of the PSR, leads to acosmism ...

How then can he take himself to reject Hegel's charges? Melamed continues: "but in spite of the charm and boldness of this interpretation, I do not think that it is sustainable"; for "the acosmist interpretation conflicts with some key doctrines of the *Ethics*."[90] But this is a point about *intent*, and it is so far from rebuttal as to be an essential *part* of Hegel's critique: "conflicts" cedes that Hegel has a strong case for an internal conflict.

Once we see that Hegel focuses on reasons, and we follow this to a distinction of the *nihilo* and affirmation abyss, what might have seemed a defense of Spinoza actually testifies to the genuinely immanent force of Hegel's critique.

3 Hegel as Taking Metaphysics Seriously to Take it Dialectically: From Shapeless Abyss to Self-Developing Thought

§3.1 Seriously but Dialectically: The Plan

I have argued that interpreters generally leave Hegel merely begging the question against Spinoza, or without reasons that would contrast with this; and I have claimed to find strong reasons. I noted above why (§0.4) I think this would make it natural to expect that there is still much to learn about how the *Logic* could get itself moving and structure itself by reasons, free of presuppositions that would beg its questions; and to expect that defense of the abyss critique might promise some help to that end.

---

[90] (2012b: 384 and n81). He also recognizes that Hegel sees the *nihilo* PSR as the root (2013: 86).

Granted, there can be no question here of a from-scratch survey of the interpretive landscape with respect to the *Logic,* let alone just the whole *Logic,* let still more alone Hegel's entire mature system. My plan here is rather to propose and initiate an interpretative approach, but with some strict limitations of focus.

First of all, I focus in detail only on the famous beginning of the *Logic*: the claim that a kind of presuppositionless thinking can begin, and must begin with consideration of pure being; and the famous claim that pure being is so indeterminate, and such an abyss, as to be nothing at all. If we can get a sense of this movement as animated by some sort of reason, then we can get a sense of how some such course of reason might get itself going without presupposition, and begin to build or structure itself by this path of negation (here, of being), or revealing self-negations (again, here, of being).

Second, aside from more specific results reached in the first two chapters on the abyss critique in the case of Spinoza (rather than, now, the case of pure being), I will draw here only on an extension of a core kind of idea from my defense of the abyss critique: Hegel takes metaphysics seriously in order to take it dialectically. That was the case with Spinoza's metaphysics above, and here it will be so with the metaphysics of pure being.

On the one hand, for those who have an easier time with Spinoza than Hegel, I hope this concluding material is a helpful point of entry into Hegel's *Logic.*

On the other hand, the point for those experienced with Hegel is not to repeat what they know, for example, that the *Logic* begins with "being"; it is to argue that my specific results and approach above, which I take to be new, (i) suggest there is significantly more to learn about how reasons could get going in the *Logic* without presupposition; (ii) provide a distinctive and helpful perspective on why the *Logic* should be so difficult; and (iii) at the same time contribute to addressing those difficulties.

The more detailed defense of reasons for a first self-reversal or negation, from being to being as nothing (§3.2), can give us at least a glimpse of how the *Logic* proceeds with reason (§3.3) *past* forms of immediacy, to mediation – and immanent critique of the metaphysics of mediation (including but not limited to the Spinoza of mediation). And that will not be complete without at least a very brief initial sense of how these results not only leave open, but can contribute to understanding of how Hegel concludes: not with a skeptical conclusion that we need either immediacy or mediation and neither works out, but by taking these negations as a way of re-centering philosophy on the method of speculative dialectical thinking, or reasoning throughout the *Logic* itself (§3.4).

§3.2 The Beginning of the Logic: The Problem and Promise of the Abyss

How could some kind of self-negating reasoning, a motor for the dialectical speculative logic to follow, get itself going in the *Logic,* without presuppositions that would merely beg the questions raised? Applying the approach above requires two steps: The first must hold off the critique of immediacy just long enough to find real strength of reason in the metaphysics of immediate, indeterminate *being* (§3.2.1). The next can then in these terms contribute towards understanding the difficulties of the *Logic*'s claim that *being is nothing,* as a problem of not begging the question; and can contribute to resolving those difficulties (§3.2.2).

3.2.1 Beginning, Without Mediation by Something Prior: Being, Pure Being

The beginning of the *Logic* claims to find reason that a systematic philosophy, thinking without presuppositions that would beg the questions to come, would begin claiming immediate grasp of "being," and "being" as indeterminate.[91] We can very roughly compare the Spinoza of immediacy, claiming an immediate grasp of the existence of God as the one substance; but not, we will see, Spinoza's own position so much as the position to which Hegel argues Spinoza is pushed, indeterminacy and all.

The text of the *Logic* is famously difficult and unusual. Just for example, it begins without a complete sentence: "*Being, pure being* – without further determination" (SL 21:68). Here I propose drawing from the account of Spinoza above to approach this:

To work by analogy, imagine this approach to Spinoza, distinguishing three levels, 1–3, in the *Ethics*. Perhaps the point in Spinoza's *Ethics* is (1) cognition of God. Some of its text would lie closer, and some farther from that point. For example, comments about Descartes in prefaces (E3Pr, E4Pr) do not bother to *demonstrate* Descartes' existence; that is unneeded insofar as such text is presumably illustrative and meant to lie far (level 3) from cognition of God (level 1); Spinoza denies that God can be conceived through a finite individual. Presumably, his strict demonstrations lie at very least *closer* to the point. But *if* the point of the demonstrations were to elicit our intellectual intuition of God's existence, then even the demonstrations would be at a level 2, distinct from something supposedly superior at level 1.[92]

---

[91] I'm grateful for exchanges with and suggestions by Anton Koch throughout this and the next section especially.

[92] Or perhaps if the point is the third kind of cognition, *scientia intuitiva*; E5P36S suggests a possible superiority of this to and the initial demonstration of monism.

That may or may not be the real Spinoza, but the point is to apply it to propose this: Hegel's *Logic* is supposed to be (level 1) purely systematic thinking. Hegel, famously, says that the beginning of this thinking is a "resolve to want to think purely," to proceed in the "absence of any presupposition" (§78); while there is debate about what this means, I will extend the above by taking it as thinking or reasoning without presuppositions that beg the questions raised. Meanwhile, some text in the *Logic* would fall (2) closer, and some (3) farther from such pure thinking. Examples of farther texts (level 3) are those I will call "commentary," often after Hegel's title "remark," which include any references to figures from history like Spinoza. The *Logic* is not about Spinoza. What I will call rather the "main" or "body" text lies closer (level 2) to its point, akin to Spinoza's demonstrations. But at least at the start, we will see that this text is not itself the systematic thinking that is the point. In Hegel I take as a paradigm of the main text the famous first paragraph in the body of the SL, on *being*, to which I now turn.[93]

Here is the first paragraph, not as something that should be understandable yet, but as reference for a close reading to come:

> *Being, pure being* – without further determination. In its indeterminate immediacy it is equal only to itself and also not unequal with respect to another; it has no difference within it, nor any outwardly. If any determination or content were posited in it as distinct, or if it were posited by this determination or content as distinct from an other, it would thereby fail to hold fast to its purity. It is pure indeterminateness and emptiness. – There is *nothing* to be intuited in it, if one can speak here of intuiting; or, it is only this pure empty intuiting itself. Just as little is anything to be thought in it, or, it is equally only this empty thinking. Being, the indeterminate immediate is in fact *nothing*, and neither more nor less than nothing. (SL 21:68–9)

So, what is the reason to begin with being? In some sense, this is the *start*. And, more to the point: this is *immediate*. So there cannot be a reason for this *in the sense of a distinct premise standing in a mediation relation of justification or ground*. So, why being?

My point here is to draw on specific results above. So here I would use the above consideration of the Spinoza of immediacy: Garrett again sees Spinoza's first proof of God's existence as inviting us to consider a seeming alternative: substance as non-existent. And our (supposedly) discovering immediately an impossibility in coherently doing so. The idea would not be to establish a distinct mediate premise, and then from there the existence of substance; it would be to recognize immediate grasp of substance as existing. So let us

---

[93] Space prohibits investigating the relation of the EL and SL and their uses of "remark."

harness our study of that idea by thinking of Hegel as inviting us to consider seeming alternatives: non-question-begging thinking starting *not* with "being" but something else. Let us say we are linguistic-turn philosophers, and we want to take *language* as first.

But, first, I think we would be meant to see that the point for such philosophy would essentially involve the idea that *there is language*. (Or at least a concept of it.) In this sense, their beginning would be complex, with language in relation to something else: that "is". Or with *being* as mediated by the specific determination or way something could be: as language. So it would not be coherent to think of the example as showing how it could make sense to begin *without being*. And we can think of beginning with being as not begging the question against others but offering them just the slightest resource that they too will need, and (for all we know now) could use: the *is*.

Second, I think we would be meant to see complex mediation *within* language. We can think of this as the distinction between subject and predicate, and think very roughly of predicates as unsaturated and incomplete and in this sense dependent (or mediated by) subjects.

I think it is not difficult to understand why Hegel would think we cannot conceive a non-question-begging thinking beginning with this complexity and mediation. He would just think that such a start would *presuppose* reality (or thought, or both) as *structured* in just the way language is structured by subject/predicate, or precisely corresponding to this. Merely presupposing the correspondence would beg the question against metaphysics that might reject this[94] – such as in the forms of Buddhist philosophy Hegel himself mentions near the start.[95] So we would be supposed to not be able to think of a truly *systematic* philosophy, resolving not to beg questions, could so begin.

Hopefully we can have a sense, then, of alternative beginnings (not "being") as complex in at very least in also requiring that "*is*" (e.g. language *is*), and complexity in the relation between whatever else (e.g. language) as determining *being*. And a sense, in this, of how results above can contribute to understanding the difficult idea of *immediate* reason to begin with just the *is* or *being*. So the EL, considering some alternative beginnings, says: "insofar as *mediation* is already present within each of these forms, they are not truly the first" (§86An). And the SL insists on beginning with the "simplest of all simples, the logical beginning" (SL 21:56).[96]

Carnap says Hegel is nonsense here (1932: 233), because confused by an ambiguity in "to be" (*sein*), between the "is" linking subject and predicate vs.

---

[94] On the lack of presupposition in this sense, I take myself to follow Houlgate (2006: e.g. 112–13).
[95] SL 21:70. For an introduction to Buddhist denials of this, Siderits 2021, ch. 5.
[96] McNulty 2022, section 2.5.

the "is" of existence; and confusing the latter with a predicate or concept, supposed "Being" (*Sein*). But I don't think Hegel is either unaware of or unfriendly to such distinctions. His point is that systematic philosophy must first try to avoid presupposing them. It is *not* that Hegel is trying to establish a foundation free of such distinctions, a mediate conclusion to ground still more. Hegel *himself* will claim that this immediacy generates a contradiction, in which careful attention would bring to light an otherwise hidden central problem for philosophy, and eventually would provide *reason* to move on to such mediation and distinctions.

Here is a way in which use of Spinoza, above, now makes sense of the unusual text at the start: Hegel must write in language. So the main text (level 2) begins in a way that gestures to something that would not presuppose subject-predicate structure, specifically by leaving out that structure: "*Being, pure being* – without further determination." The language would not be fully adequate: it cannot distinguish between a subject without predicate vs. something beyond the distinction. But it would gesture or invite us to consider the seeming alternative – beginning with just a thought of being, as distinct from being itself; or vice-versa – and in this see the point (level 1).

If there is supposed to be *reason* within this thought of immediate being, then, reason *for what?* Again, there cannot be separate premises mediating in the sense of grounding a conclusion. Nor the structure within such steps required for them to stand in inferential relations. But note what immediacy would have to do for Spinoza, if it would promise any evasion of Hegel's critique: it would have to provide, independent of steps of demonstration like those licensed by a PSR, an immediate grasp *of the existence* of substance (§1.2; 2.2–3). Here in the *Logic,* note commentary on the next page comparing Parmenides: "being is and nothing is not absolutely" (SL 21:70). Let us say that the "friends of being," or "Parmenideans" (taking this to just refer to Hegel's interpretation, regardless of the historical figure), claim an immediate grasp of being immediately ruling out the non-being of being. No mediating steps of a syllogism are required.

One great difficulty is understanding how Hegel could find a strength of reason here, in part because he so immediately turns to allege there is a contradiction here. But extensive work with Spinoza above can help, insofar as it suggests that the point is to find reason in the metaphysics of immediate being, in the sense of something strong enough to render any *external* attack inadequate, because question-begging; that leaves room for *immanent* critique, and the contradiction, to follow.

How can we understand the Parmenidean's reason as resistant to external attack? Hegel's commentary reinforces the idea that what the Parmenidean is ruling out is the non-being of being, by pointing to a Kantian objection to an "ontological proof." Think of a Kantian saying: *This Parmenidean claim of immediate access to 'being is' would merely be a form of ontological argument (OA), even if it is unusual taking God as just Being. Still, it falls to "Kantian criticism" of the "ontological proof"* (SL 21:76). *Like any OA, it is left clarifying a mere concept, like a concept of <being>, and this can never establish that being is, or exists, because – as Kant famously holds – being is not a predicate that could be added to such a concept.*[97] (Carnap's worry about Hegel's "Being" follows Kant's famous claim.[98])

Note that I do not introduce the comparison to an OA in my own name. Whatever it might promise, it threatens much distortion: immediate being is too immediate to be an "argument" in the natural sense of conclusions mediated by premises; there is here no determinate traditional concept of God, only Being; and we are about to see why Hegel thinks *this* reason could not support God in any determinate sense.[99]

The question, then, is why Hegel thinks this Kantian attack would be, *applied to the Parmenidean thought*, merely external and question-begging. The answer is not difficult to see: The friend of immediate being is from the start putting forward the view that, *for immediate being*, "concept" and "being are *unseparated* and *inseparable*" (SL 21:77). For a *reply* it would be philosophically unsatisfying to assume the contrary, to *begin* claiming there is always a distinction between concept and object, essence and existence, or similar.[100]

Those favorable to Kant or Carnap will want to know why their Parmenidean opponent got to speak first, subjecting their point to the standards for a *reply*. But here is where we see the reason for the indeterminacy: We have noted Hegel's reasons for thinking that consideration of simple *being* must come first. The strength of reason in the face of Kantianism could not attach to any claim for a God in any sense of being determined in some way, as wise, good, etc.

Further, imagine the above resistance to Kant were claimed for any determinate concept of God, say, God as F. This would seem to distinguish God's existence from a concept or essence of God, and lose the strength of reason in denying such a distinction before Kant can then reply.

---

[97] A598/B626. [98] 1932: 233.
[99] Any more determinate sense of "God" that Hegel might come to later would be via taking this seriously, but specifically as undermining itself, or via dialectic (not supposed immediate grasp).
[100] Cf. McNulty 2022: 106. More space would be needed here to argue that external defense of concept/object would still draw on a presupposed distinction.

For pure being, we got at least a sense of a reason it would come first. But to take such being seriously suggests that its friends should *themselves* accept, welcome, or even insist on the total *indeterminacy* of being.

Some might object with confusion about the topic: Is this an indeterminacy of being *itself*, or rather of a *grasp* of being (a thought, intuition, concept, etc.)? Again, the point is to try to think independently of assuming such a distinction. Again, the text on indeterminacy gestures at this: Of being, "[t]here is *nothing* to be intuited in it, if one can speak here of intuiting; or, it is only this pure empty intuiting itself" (GW 21:69; he then adds the same for *thought* as well as intuition). *If* we could here distinguish grasp from object, we could say the topic is an immediate *grasp* of being as indeterminate; or that *being itself* is indeterminate. I think the text withholds ascent from the antecedent, and thereby gestures behind the distinction, as it were.

We can understand in these terms something implicit above: Say we make a claim of immediate *grasp* of something's existence, which is to say: without mediation by steps of argument or syllogism. The *Logic* finds reason that we cannot resist taking this as well as a commitment about *what that something itself must be in itself* (for such appeal to provide any reason): it is simple, without standing in mediation relations with something else, or having any mediation relations within. Immediacy in grasp, and in itself. The supposed distinction collapses here; immediacy and indeterminacy encompass any distinction between sides here.[101] Immediacy would eliminate determinacy in all forms, prior to the Spinozist having a chance to define attributes or modes; if they want a substance that mediates modes "in" it, then they will need arguments for this that turn on mediation.

I emphasize that there is not meant to be here a stable conclusion established, a Parmenideanism accepted as a basis from which to mediate or ground further inferences about being, making Hegel's results a subvariety of Parmenideanism. This is rather the occasion for the dialectical reversal to which I now turn.

3.2.2 Deeper Into the Abyss: Being is Nothing

This section seeks to understand how the main text's first paragraph finds reason to reverse the starting point of the *Logic,* concluding that being "is in fact *nothing*, and neither more nor less than nothing" (SL 21:68–9). The above

---

[101] So the beginning certainly cannot be non-metaphysical, or any retreat from the metaphysical. *If* we define "metaphysics" as limited to only one determinately distinct subdomain of philosophy, it would follow so far into metaphysics as to come out beyond it. But I think it natural to recognize such concern with being as one way of understanding "metaphysics," even if this comes out larger, as it were, than on some other definitions. Again, I try not to make anything substantive here rest on arguments about any supposedly single best use of the term.

should initially heighten the sense of difficulty here, or give a useful perspective on why matters are so difficult: insofar as the Parmenidean has reason to welcome indeterminacy, and yet presumably *not* the idea that being is nothing, this is a specific and specifically large gulf. It separates where Hegel has reason to start, and where he claims reason to go. To put it another way, we have just seen the most general case that Spinoza, if appealing to immediacy, would lose all determinations: but how could we possibly give *immanent* critique of a Spinoza who welcomed this, namely, Parmenides as Hegel sees him?

It is of course not unusual to note difficulties in this move; Houlgate says, "[o]f all Hegel's statements in the *Logic*," being is nothing "*is the* one that has perhaps invited the most ridicule ... ." But results above allow clarifying a sense in which the difficulty is greater for Hegel's statement than Houlgate says here: "[i]n Hegel's view ... it is trivially true: pure being is utterly indeterminate and vacuous and as such is completely indistinguishable from sheer and utter nothingness" (2006: 264). Results above suggest rather this: What would be vacuous would be the claim that there is nothing *by way of determinations* in Parmenidean being; but the text moves from there to an idea about what being *is*, not what it is indistinguishable from. It is *"nothing"*: "Nichts," with the capitalization of a noun, suggesting this is not just *nothing by way of* determinations.[102]

Now that we take more seriously the Parmenidean friends of being, we can see them as having an obvious objection to Hegel, along these lines: *Yes, when we look to being from a perspective that can only think in terms of determinations, we indeed find nothing ("nichts") in it. But that is because a determination is a limit. Not because being in itself is nothing ("Nichts"). There is too much of being for it to be determined, as it were, rather than too little.*

Paradigmatically insufficient attempts to defend Hegel, by the lights of the *Logic*, would include those beginning with: *everything involves negation* (§2.2.2). Or if we *begin* by taking proper philosophy to concern specifically a question like: *how could there be any determinate being?* Or: *how could an object be determinately knowable or judgeable?* The idea would have been to infer that being, to be determinately what it itself is, would require a reference – a negative reference – to non-being, or nothing. But these responses make external presuppositions that Parmenideans would, so far, have no reason to accept.

My position is that this seeming gulf cannot be dispelled without putting the approach above to use by no longer trying to exclude from supposedly proper

---

[102] SL 21:69; for more on this problem: Koch 2022: 66.

philosophy Parmenideanism, or the position to which Spinoza is pushed, or indeterminate being; only by instead taking it yet *more* seriously as philosophy. The idea is that the Parmenideans' immediacy reason actually supports yet more: a kind of monism, in ruling out there being any distinctions.[103] In my view, this is at least part of what Hegel means in insisting that philosophy must begin with Spinoza (carried through, as Hegel sees it):

> When one begins to philosophize one must be first a Spinozist. The soul must bathe itself in the aether of this single substance, in which everything one believed true has perished (VGP 20:165/3:257).[104]

I think Hegel's Parmenides-inspired reason for this dissolution of distinctions is supposed to be this: *If* we take seriously the Parmenidean *being is,* then we seem to take seriously the other side of this as well: "being is and nothing is not absolutely" (SL 21:70). If we immediately rule out the non-being of being, so too the being of non-being. But distinctions *internal* to being would involve there *being the non-being* of something on one side of it, that is present on the other side. Or, there *being nothing* of this on one side. Matters would be similar with an *external* distinction between being and something else. The something else presumably *is not being,* and our immediacy reason should rule that out. Our main text's first paragraph *has already, prior to the equation with nothing*, denied that there are any distinctions in either respect: "Being ... has no difference within it, nor any outwardly" (SL 21:68–9).[105]

But the twist is that the Parmenideans' own reason *now eliminates their objection to Hegel's move to equate being and nothing*. They cannot allow any *distinction* between a limited perspective (thinking only in determinations) vs. being in itself. So they cannot say that, from a merely limited perspective, there is nothing to being, without threat to being in itself. If it made sense to speak of perspective, they could allow only the perspective of being. And so our taking them seriously contributes to our understanding that there is nowhere else to lodge the "nothing" (*nichts*) found, but in being itself: it is "Nothing" (*Nichts*).

---

[103] On this Parmenideanism as a form of monism, Della Rocca (2020). In seeing difficulties for Hegel in the need to take this seriously, I follow Koch (2022). I am arguing we can see work done here by something more internal to Parmenideanism than what Koch calls his *"more external reflections"* on this particular point (78).

[104] Other meanings could be seen here, for example, reference to the development of the history of German Idealism, and the role of Schelling and perhaps Fichte taking Spinoza seriously. I think, if so, then these are layers of meaning additional to my point here, but I won't rest weight on the passage.

[105] Della Rocca sees this as monism (2020: 1), even though it would also deny there is *one* as distinct from *more*.

Hegel and Spinoza 51

Again, this is not meant to be a stable conclusion to mediate or ground further inference; it is the beginning of a long path of dialectic, and is meant to be fully and adequately understood in terms of how that path proceeds (§3.4).

Finally, there is much else to be said about this paragraph. What I have argued here is that results and the approach above provide a useful perspective on the difficulties here, the difficulty of finding a genuinely immanent and non-question-begging form of reason to start the *Logic* moving; *and* they contribute to resolving those difficulties.

§3.3 A Seriously/Dialectically Approach to the Promise and Indeterminacy-Failure of Mediation

Space constrains me to look away from the details at this point. But consider an objection: My approach works by taking reasons for metaphysics seriously, arguing that this is necessary to Hegel's dialectic. An objection would be that *this* Hegel could never escape ending up with at least some form of the general kind of metaphysics he sees in Spinoza.

I think my results here do not foreclose but open approaches to Hegel's more comprehensive break with the kind of metaphysics he sees in Spinoza. To defend this, I will sketch one such approach that is open: the one I favor. I do so not with the presumption that there is space to adequately develop and defend it, but to answer the worry that such approaches have been foreclosed. I proceed with a sense of how the first reversal, above, might provide reason further driving the *Logic* and structuring its three parts (§3.3.1); and this might help in understanding how the *Logic* might break with not only the metaphysics of immediacy but also that of mediation, including but not limited to the details in Spinoza (§3.3.2).

3.3.1 Preparing for Reasons Structuring the Logic

Hegel characterizes "dialectic" as essential to the form of reason animating the *Logic,* involving the uncovering of "contradictions" and their "resolution" (e.g. EL §11).[106] So it is not surprising that he sees a contradiction in the result that *being is nothing.*

All I want to point out here is how the above might contribute to the understanding of why this should be a contradiction: We have found and taken seriously an immediacy reason to deny distinctions between being and

---

[106] I think it true, but not an objection to this, to point out that Hegel also allows that there can be true contradictions. I think it a problem for *any* study of Hegel on contradiction to explain how he can both (i) take contradictions to force further development of the *Logic*, and (ii) take some contradictions as true. My last stab at this was my 2015, Ch. 7.

anything else. In this sense, it is reason to hold that *there is only being*. But now we get something further and problematic out of the idea that *being is nothing*. We get the idea that *there is nothing*. And that is a help: We need only get some sense of why there being nothing would have to involve there being something.

Consider the matter in this way: Say *my pen is on my desk*. Perhaps we can make sense of this entirely in terms of the ordinary objects: my pen and my desk. But it seems different to think that *there is nothing*. There is nothing like the pen, or desk. We could try to do without any such objects to be referred to in the claim – a desk or pen or even "the nothing" – by just thinking that there is a fact, namely, the fact that there is nothing. But if there is nothing, there is no fact.[107] In Hegel's terms, the idea is that we must contradict ourselves in distinguishing being and nothing (in taking there to be something), and yet identify them for reasons above (SL 21:77).

But have my results then foreclosed understanding how this contradiction, or this kind of contradiction, could power the rest of the *Logic?* Again I think not. To just show that an approach is open, I would again sketch mine. I would note that Hegel's commentary redescribes the reason against stopping with immediate being as a *challenge* specifically for those who would resist the equation of being and nothing:

> ... the challenge to state what, then, is being, and what is nothing. Those who resist ... let them declare whereof they speak, that is, let them advance a definition of being and nothing, and let them demonstrate that it is correct. (SL 21:79–80)

In particular, say we wish to ignore Hegel's results and go on philosophizing; this would no doubt mean taking the objects of our philosophy to *be*. But the *Logic* found reason to begin as it does, and found reason to think this would be – barring further development – a contradiction that precludes a stable conclusion. So it would then be question-begging to take there to be some other object for philosophy – language, or whatever – without answering Hegel's challenge.

Granted, in the pure systematic thinking of Hegel's *Logic* – level 1, as it were – we are never supposed to confront this problem as such.[108] One reason is that the *Logic* never encounters its negations without supposedly already finding something more developed. In the present case, Hegel thinks this is the movement between being and nothing, and back again, which he calls "becoming." And that of course will not be a conclusion but an occasion for further movement.

---

[107] Thanks here to Koch and his (2019). Note I did not introduce a general metaphysics of facts in my name; it is offered as a way to avoid contradiction in this special case, and it fails.

[108] Thanks to Daniel Leblanc here.

Another reason is that the very point is that there is so far no stable way to think being, and so strictly speaking no way for purely systematic thought to pose the problem.[109]

What I want to propose about this is just that discussion above of immediacy can help: Perhaps Spinoza invites us to entertain substance as nonexistent, expecting we will immediately rule this out – rather than as conclusion mediated by premises. I suggested we think of the beginning of the *Logic* this way, as inviting us to entertain seemingly alternative beginnings. And then we could see each step of the *Logic* as inviting us to entertain the idea of concluding there; but, at each step short of the end, we would be expected to see that we would be taking something to be, but could not yet, due to the contradiction. And that would reveal what powers further progress.

This approach could then connect the broadest three-part structure of the *Logic* by noting that, at transitions to the second and third parts, it states the ideas to be considered in those parts as offering accounts of "the truth of being."[110] Next, the "Doctrine of Essence," reason for and then immanent reason against its first words: "The *truth* of *being* is *essence*" (SL 11:241).

3.3.2 The Metaphysics of Mediation: The Truth of Being is Essence

In the broadest sense, the kind of view considered in the "Doctrine of Essence" is unremarkable: it is unremarkable to find philosophers' projects organized around a mediation or dependence relation like that between grounded and ground, conditioned and condition, justified and justifier, and so on. My aim in this section is to argue that results above have not foreclosed the *Logic* having reason to reject both the metaphysics of immediacy in general, and the metaphysics of mediation (including, but not limited to, Spinoza's case). Again, I argue this by pointing out an approach that is not foreclosed.

To begin with, then, Hegel thinks some reason is needed to organize philosophy around mediation. So consider again the problem of being and nothing: there turns out to be no determinate distinction; and that turns out not just to be something that many (including Spinoza) would reject; it is supposed to turn out to be a contradiction forcing further movement. There are *many* ways of doing without mediation or priority-involving dependence – many ways considered

---

[109] For the same reason, although greatly influenced by throughout by McNulty and his criticisms of my earlier work, I do not agree that Hegel accepts "ontological argument" claiming that being is "necessarily instantiated" (2022: 98), to "transmit" (30) to further logical categories. Similarly, I would resist suggestion in Houlgate that the *Logic* has found its object, being, and need only watch it unfold itself (e.g. 2006: 60ff.).

[110] E.g. WL 11:241; §88, §159.

in the first part of the *Logic*. They are in many respects different than the first step, above. But we could approach the difficulties here in terms of the idea that determinate distinction is supposed to be lacking so long as mediation is excluded. For example, Hegel quickly comes to the idea of a supposedly determinate "something"; he argues not just that it requires reference to what lies beyond its determinate limits, but that this "other" is no different than the "something" – again, determinate distinction lost.[111]

Contrast philosophers' ordinary ideas of the topic in "Essence": priority-involving explanatory dependence relations, like causality. The promise, at least, is of a different kind of determinate distinction: between the priority of cause, and the posteriority of effect.[112] So the *Logic* invites us to consider whether it could conclude with some such mediation relation, and not continue to fall into an abyss of indeterminacy. For reasons above, this would mean appeal to causal priority in order "to state what, then, is being" (SL 21:79–80), without falling into indeterminacy and back into the initial contradiction. And the result is not *so* unusual as one might have expected for Hegel; an example would be accounting for being in terms of causality in the sense of an Eleatic principle: *to be is to have causal power*.

Or, to think in terms of ground, Hegel's approach is to consider something like: *to be is to have a ground*. We would be supposed to think *nothing* as distinct by subtracting the ground. Insofar as ground/grounded would be a determinate distinction, we would find through it a determinate account of "the truth of being." And I think this is how the *Logic* understands the promise of principle of sufficient "reason" (*Grund*): it "means nothing but this: Anything which *is*, is to be considered *to exist* not as an *immediate*, but as a *posited* ... " (11:293). So here the *Logic* would find *reason for* the PSR: to do without it (or at least anything like it, concerning priority-involving dependence) would fall back into an abyss contradiction of indeterminacy.

Broadening out from grounding, Hegel takes the general idea of being as mediated as this: being is what *results* (in the sense of some mediation relation) from a source that is *prior*. Hegel's most general term for the *source* of being is "essence" (*Wesen*); he notes that *gewesen* is the past-participle of the verb *to be*, suggesting that being is what flows from something prior. And that is what the approach here suggests is meant by the first words of Part Two in the SL: "The *truth* of *being* is *essence*" (11:241).

---

[111] SL 21:102ff.

[112] Hegel's version of the transition seems to take the failed versions of immediacy as revealing themselves as something like modes depending on underlying substrate or substance (SL 21:381)

If we have that reason for the metaphysics of mediation, the way is open for approaches to both why a reason against this should be difficult, and how to nonetheless find its own reasons turning against it.

As to the difficulty, it is familiar to note this sort of Hegelian worry about a philosophy of grounding, for example: to be a ground is to have a grounded (Hegel claims); but then the grounded *grounds* the ground being a ground. So the determinate priority distinction between ground and grounded is lost.

But what could be the reason for thinking that: *to be a ground is to have a grounded*? The approach above suggests this is not an easy case to make: approximately no philosophy built around priority-involving mediation would admit this.

To illustrate, Hegel engages in "Essence" with various forms of Spinozism built around dependence relations, such as causality. But we could not meet such a Spinozist simply with a claim that substance cannot cause anything, without itself being dependent on that something, conceived through it, and no longer substance. They would see this as external, and question-begging.

Can we argue that all determination is negation, so that to be substance-as-cause would involve not being whatever is caused by substance, thus depending on the latter? But we have seen this principle to beg the question against Spinozists (§3.2.2). So we have yet no adequate reason for thinking there is any internal difficulty in the metaphysics of mediation.

But results here also can contribute to approaches to a genuinely internal reason. Here is an approach: Say we have a reason for a metaphysics appealing to ground-grounded "to state what, then, is being" (SL 21:79). But then *this* (even if not necessarily any reference to ground) does seem to require an account of *what it is to ground,* or *what it is to be a ground.* The grounding theorist would not be able to reply that we have *immediate* access to the priority and so distinction of ground to grounded: immediacy would have already been shown to force elimination of determinate distinction.[113] So an account would seem required. And such a metaphysics of mediation would have no something else, X, below grounding to reach for in its account – else it would be a metaphysics of X, rather than grounding. To appeal to ground to account for ground would be immediacy. So nothing would be left but to account for ground except in terms of the grounded, saying something like: to ground is to have a grounded. And *then* the Hegelian charge would stick: ground would need grounding in the grounded; the priority difference would disappear. In Hegel's terms, ground "is ground only insofar as it is ground of something" (§121An).

---

[113] §3.2. Compare the contemporary metaphysics of grounding taking it as primitive (e.g. Schaffer 2009).

Why might this be a contradiction? The idea would be that we need to affirm ground as distinct from and prior to grounded, to avoid the abyss contradiction of indeterminacy. And yet to so use grounding would turn out to deny that very priority distinction. Compare something Hegel says of cause-effect: "the inseparability is one determination, the diversity the other, that is contradiction" (VL 168/23,2:770).

With respect to the forms of Spinozism considered in this part of the *Logic*, they would be considered in light of previous results: A Spinoza of mediation would require an account of what it is to be. And would have to seek this in a mediation or priority relation. Then it is easier to see, as above, why such a Spinozism might be vulnerable to the charge that its supposed priority relation would invert or collapse.

This would be the *Logic*'s most strict and general version of an abyss critique of the metaphysics of the PSR or grounding, finding there indeterminacy and contradiction: an argument that making such mediation central eliminates all determinacy (modes, attributes, whatever).

Space allows only this glance at this one form of the many problems in "Essence," and the large family of mediation relations there.[114] My aim here has only been to show that results above open an approach to this: On the one hand, finding serious reason for the metaphysics of mediation in the treatment of being and nothing above gives a distinctive perspective on why non-question-begging critique of mediation should be so difficult; on the other, the same treatment can contribute to resolving the difficulties: the reason for the metaphysics of mediation would also force indeterminacy and contradiction.

§3.4 A Seriously/Dialectically Approach to the Conclusion of the Logic: Self-Negation and Self-Developing Thought

Again, space prohibits adequately developing and defending an account of the *Logic's* conclusion in its third part, "The Doctrine of the Concept." But consider an objection to the above: Say Hegel takes the metaphysics of immediacy and mediation as seriously as I have argued he does. The objection would be that he is then at an impasse: either mediation or no mediation (immediacy); the possibilities seem exhausted. And my approach has excluded finding relief in the idea that the *Logic* simply pursues some form of philosophy from the perspective of which all such metaphysics – whether of immediacy or mediation – is naïve, outdated, and so a matter of philosophical indifference. To show that my claims above do not foreclose approaches to the further

---

[114] My previous gloss (2015: 215f); I'm now influenced by Knappik's take on the kinds of problems (2016: 767).

problem, I will sketch one: the one I favor, on which results here contribute not just to understanding the difficulty, but also to addressing it.

Here is some Hegelian terminology for the problem: sometimes Hegel uses "dialectical" for a *negative* side of his method: eliminating thoughts via supposedly internal contradiction. In such places, he construes his method as dialectical-*speculative*, where the "speculative" is meant to emphasize that dialectic generates a positive result (§80–82).

The beginning of the "Doctrine of the Concept" provides a kind of tagline for what would be generated or derived, beyond the distinction of immediacy and mediation: "development" (*Entwicklung*) (§161). As a rough image – merely an image – Hegel's notes offer the development of a plant from seed to maturity.[115] On the one hand, "development" would no longer distinguish two relata, as in a mediation relation: rather one thing, the plant, would develop *itself*. On the other hand, development would preserve the determinacy of a directed process of one *stage,* itself *distinct* from the next. So, Hegel says, "what are differentiated are at the same time immediately posited as identical with one another and with the whole" (EL §161; Kreines 2015: 216).

I do not think this beginning in itself solves Hegel's problem, or is meant to. That would seem to require some sense of why or how a plant develops. Is the earlier stage the *cause* of the later plant?[116] This seems to fall back into mediation taking cause as distinct from effect. Hegel would think causal thinking inadmissible to the activity of a plant.[117] But so far the alternative way to grasp this would be to claim an immediate grasp; Hegel has argued that an immediacy reason forces elimination of determinacy.

So matters are not complete at the beginning. What about the end ("The Absolute Idea")? Here Hegel comes to reflect on the "method" of thinking throughout the *Logic*. What kind of conclusion could that be? What would follow up the results and approach above would be to say that systematic thought or reason – as pursued in the *Logic*, through dialectical negations or reversals – finds *itself* as completely self-developing, and offers our first adequate grasp of that self-development.

Here is the idea, in terms of results above: I gave a specific account here of how that method would find reason to begin as it does – with pure being – *without presuppositions.* And an account of how it would find reason in this to

---

[115] §161Zu; §166Zu; GW 23,2: 624–5. I'm drawing on my previous account of this as distinct from earlier topics (2015: 215ff).

[116] Or, if we reach for an Aristotelian view, we would still *distinguish* matter in *relation* to form, as prior – or actuality to potentiality.

[117] I've discussed this in 2015, ch. 3, but I now think that material insufficiently appreciates the difficulty stated here.

proceed or move forward *to* nothingness, and in this provide reason to move further. I have proposed an account of this as reason to move away from any form of immediacy, to mediation. If there is reason in these moves, then there would be a sense in which, as such dialectical reason, it constructs a series of determinately distinct steps, or develops itself in this way.

To see Hegel's terms for this we have to note what he calls "the" concept (*Begriff*). There is *a* concept of something like matter, for example.[118] But *the* concept I take to be the concept of thought, or the kind of thinking pursued in the *Logic* itself. The end of the *Logic* reflects on method and claims to have shown that "the concept" in this sense is self-developing:

> ... what is to be considered as method here is only the movement of the concept itself ... its movement is the universal absolute activity, the self-determining and self-realizing movement. (SL 12:238)[119]

We can see a similar idea in Hegel's lecture notes on the beginning of the *Logic*. The idea is that this structure of the *Logic* cannot be assumed at the start, but must be demonstrated within:

> ... the justification or proof of it can only result from the completed treatment of thinking itself ... in philosophy, demonstrating is equivalent to showing how the object makes itself – through and out of itself – into what it is. (§83Z)

So the systematic thought pursued in the *Logic* would, just in being a course of reason or demonstration, *make itself what it is* – giving itself the structure developed in the *Logic*.

On the one hand, this self-development would not itself be explained in terms of reason in the sense of mediation of distinct relata, like an initially established premise, to mediate or ground further conclusions. Each established conclusion would be supposed to have negated itself. For example, in a sense it was established that "[t]he *truth* of *being* is *essence*" (SL 11:241). But the second "Essence" would find this undercutting itself (§3.3.2).

On the other hand, this self-development would *also* not be such as to be graspable immediately. It would be what it is only in finding such immediacy – and everything to follow – to be self-overcoming or negating. Nor would it be indeterminate like immediate being: it would distinguish stages of itself, making itself into determinately what it is.

This form of reason would be dialectical: moving by self-negations. And dialectical-speculative: finding in double negation an affirmative result, and in the end, finding *itself* as its affirmative result.

---

[118] Both on this case and on concepts in this sense, see Kreines (2015).
[119] On this cf. Siep 2018: 659f., 735ff.

Granted, my approach has imposed a difficult constraint here. In particular, this conclusion would have to provide an account of *being*. Is an approach to this open? Yes: we can take the conclusion to be something like this: to be is to be some form or stage of the self-development of thought, or absolute self-negation.

That is of course wildly ambitious, but I think any approach will need something like this: any approach must make sense of the claim at the transition to the final "Doctrine of the Concept" that "[t]he concept is .... the truth of being ... " (§159). And this would make sense of another part of the passage above, from the conclusion of the *Logic*. We know the method of the *Logic* at this point, since we have been following it throughout. But:

> ... what is to be considered as method here is only the movement of the *concept* itself. We already know the nature of this movement, but it now has, *first*, the added significance that **the *concept is all***, and that its movement is the *universal absolute activity*, the self-determining and self-realizing movement. (SL 12:238; bold emphasis mine)

If what it is to be is to be some form of "the concept," then, "the *concept is all*."

We would be meant to be invited to retrospectively grasp in these terms all that came before. What would we then say about the activity of that plant after all? The adequate grasp of its activity would be neither causal nor immediate, but grasp of it as at least some form of the self-developing activity of thought.

What would we say about pure being? We would understand what we are trying to say of some X, if we tried to say that it *is* but there is nothing more to it: we would be saying that *only* the thought or category that comes first in thought, immediately, applies to it: first in a series that eventually finds itself as self-developing. And we can understand what it means to say that being is nothing: something about which we could *only* say it "is" would just be nothing, since we cannot really separate the category of being from the later self-development, or grasp it as anything but a *stage* connected to that development.

Or consider the finite. I noted above the idea that thought develops entirely according to its own "concept." This leaves open taking *finite* things to have a concept, but not to be *completely* determined by concept of their own. What is it to be finite is to be, but incompletely, the self-development of thought. I would look to this text:

> ... finite things are finite because, and to the extent that, they do not possess the reality of their concept completely within them but are in need of other things for it. (SL 12:175)

How to categorize such a conclusion? One could *roughly* approach it by seeing self-developing thought as Hegel's *replacement* for Spinoza's substance. And especially for Spinoza's attempts to portray substance, in terms of causality, as a self-cause or *causa sui*.[120] But this would not be the most philosophically perspicuous way to conclude:

For one thing, Hegel's ultimate point cannot exactly be that everything is "in" one thing, whether substance or thought or anything else. That would rest the weight at the end of the day on the relation of something being "in" something else: a form of mediation.

Further, imagine concluding an account of Spinoza with a comparison between substance and an ocean. The comparison can help with rough orientation, but is not an adequate conclusion: substance cannot be adequately conceived through the finite. And Spinoza thinks we misunderstand what substance is if we misunderstand the *reasons* for it as inferences from the finite. I think there is even more cause to think this about the ultimate object of Hegel's *Logic*, insofar as that object seems to *be* the reason that animates the *Logic*. Since I do not think that Spinoza reasons in Hegel's double self-negating dialectical/speculative manner, I do not think it can be most adequate to think of Hegel's alternative as a version of Spinoza's philosophy.

Would it be a form of "monism"? *Not*, again, in the most natural sense of holding at base that everything is "in" one thing. Nor in a Parmenidean sense of asserting an immediate grasp of something that rules out anything else. Beyond that is tricky. Since Hegel does not use the term "monism" in this way, there is no need to square results here with his use of it. It would be worth making a study trying to find a sense of the term in which it would be philosophically perspicacious, but I do not try this here.

Would Hegel have overcome of "metaphysics," or found a new kind of metaphysics? What I think is easy to say is this: It is not just a version of metaphysics in the sense of an immediate concern with being; nor just a version of metaphysics in a sense fixed by a mediation relation: metaphysics as concerned with what grounds what, or any ultimate ground. About "metaphysics" in any such sense, we should say that Hegel moves through and beyond "metaphysics". But I have also argued here that Hegel's cannot be any form of philosophy that has any character (whether we call this a "non-metaphysical" character, or a "critical" rather than "pre-critical" spirit) that leads to taking those very kinds of metaphysics to be naïve, outdated, and a matter of philosophical indifference; it is animated by taking them seriously as philosophy.

---

[120] See Hegel's treatment of Spinoza as pointing the way at the transition to "The Concept," but unable to follow due to attachment to mediation; EL: §153.

I suspect Hegel's serious engagement with such forms of metaphysics suggests there are also philosophically perspicacious senses in which he would be uncovering a new kind of "metaphysics", of absolute negation, or similar; but nothing here hangs on this topic for future consideration.

<u>Does Hegel fall into his own version of the abyss critique?</u> My results make some progress here, and for remaining puzzles have not made them any more difficult than they would otherwise be. On my account the abyss critique of Spinoza targets appeals to immediacy (§2.2) and use of the PSR as in the *nihilo* form, requiring for everything existing a cause (§2.1). I have argued that Hegel takes both seriously, *but ultimately critically.* He is not tied to these as forms of reason for his conclusion; he is tied to them as thoughts that undermine themselves, pointing beyond themselves. So my results contribute to showing him free from concern that both kinds of considerations do very much threaten the abyss. He is not on the hook for finding causes for the existence of everything or else eliminating.

Granted, there are more tricky issues that can arise here; but I do not think my approach has inflamed them.[121] We could say that, on the account of Hegel here, something PSR-adjacent is true: nothing is brutely *what* it is. For self-developing thought would make itself what it is; and such thought is all. But I have suggested why Hegel would not think this threatens the finite: I have just noted the account I think Hegel gives of *what* it is to be finite; that is neither left brute, nor eliminated.

Does my approach foreclose doing justice to the importance of *freedom* in Hegel's sense of his difference from Spinoza? I think not. What I set aside, *following Hegel,* was the idea of appealing to freedom as reason against Spinoza. But I have just suggested an account on which legitimate internal engagement with the kind of metaphysics in Spinoza gives us access to a form of freedom: "the self-determining and self-realizing movement" of the concept, or thought (SL 12:238).

Have I unjustly ignored the importance, for Hegel, of the idea that *all determination is negation*? No. What I set aside was the idea that he argues on this basis against Spinoza, or really any form of metaphysics that would have reason to deny the claim. On the approach here, Hegel comes to this through more immanent engagements with all that metaphysics. The determinacy of thinking would be the self-negation of the thoughts considered along the way; and such thinking is *all*; so, all determinacy would involve negation.

At this point, space constrains me to turn to conclusions.

---

[121] I have used this idea in defense of Hegel against an abyss critique targeting his transition from the *Logic* to the *Philosophy of Nature* in my 2024.

Hegel and Spinoza: From the Shapeless Abyss to Self-Developing Thought

I have not here tried to develop let alone defend an adequate account of the end of the *Logic*. Nor of everything in the *Logic*. Space made these tasks impossible from the start.

And I should add that I have also not yet dipped into the rest of Hegel's system. We could roughly compare something in Spinoza: After the defense of monism, the *Ethics* turns at the beginning of Part II to the attributes of extension and thought. The place to begin in Hegel's system, to compare discussion of extension and thought would be the rest of the system, in the *Philosophy of Nature*, and the *Philosophy of Spirit*. Issues related to the above would arise there; for example, is Hegel's treatment of spatio-temporal nature itself a kind of "monism" of that domain?[122]

But I have kept this book within its limits by focusing on the abyss critique, and here what was needed in Spinoza was the proof of monism in Part I, prior to the specifics about extension and thought; and that has made most salient issues most parallel to this, in Hegel's *Logic*. About the rest I have at least explained why I would not worry that the *Logic* need find a cause of the existence of nature, or else eliminate it.

So let me return to my two organizing aims.

The first was to defend Hegel's abyss critique of Spinoza. I argued that interpreters generally have left Hegel in his engagement with Spinoza without reasons, in the sense of being without a non-question-begging case against Spinoza. Sometimes interpreters note the failure, and sometimes they do not.

But I have shown that interpreters are wrong about this: Hegel has a genuinely immanent critique, and it is powerful.

A first key is that Hegel focuses on Spinoza's *reasons* animating Spinoza's substance monism. And so my overarching aim here organizes together my account of Spinoza's reasons for monism (§1), and my (§2) defense of the case that *these very reasons* threaten to force the elimination of determinacy. Hegel knows that Spinoza does not intend to entirely eliminate it: that is not a rebuttal, but part of the critique, which alleges an internal conflict.

But the real unnoticed key is that a focus on reasons allows a distinction between reasons of mediation (like the PSR) and those of immediacy – corresponding to the topics of the first two parts of Hegel's *Logic,* each of which includes many comments on Spinoza. Hegel has a case that *both* force an indeterminate abyss. With this in hand we can see that attempted defenses of Spinoza tend to reinforce the strength of the critique: Spinoza

---

[122] It is often alleged that an acosmism problem arises for Hegel concerning the transition to nature; I use my approach to respond in my (2024).

can be read in ways designed to dodge one side of the attack, but doing so will tend to inflame the other.

The second overarching aim was meant to organize those two chapters together with a third. The idea here is that interpreters' not having solved the problem of a non-question-begging form of reason in the abyss critique of *Spinoza*, should make it natural to expect that there is still much to learn about Hegel's *Logic*, especially concerning difficulties about how some form of reason could get itself going there without drawing on presuppositions that would beg the questions to be raised. And the same should make it natural to expect that the defense of the abyss critique here has much to offer concerning those difficulties.

I have responded by drawing on specific results concerning Spinoza, and the general seriously/dialectically approach to Hegel, in an interpretation of how reasons in the *Logic* can get themselves moving, into their first self-reversal: the first body paragraph's identification of being with nothing. On the one hand, the seriously/dialectically approach provides a distinctive perspective on why the challenge here is so difficult, and the text so unusual: by finding a form of reason in immediate, indeterminate being – and the kind of position to which Hegel argues Spinoza is pushed – the challenge is raised of how to respond to this reason without begging the question. But, by the same token, this can contribute to an understanding of how this section solves its problems: taking the metaphysics of immediate being even more seriously shows that it overcomes an otherwise obvious objection to Hegel's movement to the idea that being is nothing.

From there, space has constrained me to leave the *details* of the *Logic* behind. But I have fielded the objection that my seriously/dialectically approach would foreclose accounts of how Hegel could critique of the metaphysics of mediation, beyond just the specifics of Spinoza. I have shown that my results leave open approaches, by sketching mine: drawing on results here to find Hegel's sense of the real reason *for* the metaphysics of mediation, and how that reason would turn against itself in a kind of abyss critique. Finally, I have fielded a similar objection, a worry that if my seriously/dialectically Hegel could get this far, this would foreclose approaches to any conclusion of the *Logic* getting beyond an impasse between the metaphysics of immediacy and mediation. I have shown that approaches are not foreclosed, again by sketching one that puts results here to work: It remains open to find a conclusion for the *Logic* in its turn to the very form of reasoning whose initiation is treated in detail here: reasons as a process of self-negating and self-developing thought. Because Hegel is so careful to not beg questions, it would perhaps not have been appropriate to begin with this, final point; but hopefully at the end this book can begin to claim its true subtitle: *Hegel and Spinoza: From Shapeless Abyss to Self-Developing Thought.*

Sources

Abbreviations

Spinoza

Passages of the *Ethics* are cited with an E, followed by the Part number, and then as follows: A axiom; C corollary; D demonstration or definition depending on context; P proposition; S scholium; L Lemma.

CW = Curley, Edwin. The Collected Works of Spinoza. 2 vols (Princeton: Princeton University Press, 1985 and 2016). Cited by volume : page.

Kant

Ak.= Immanuel Kant. 1902–. *Kants gesammelte Schriften.* Berlin: Walter de Gruyter.

A/B = Immanuel Kant. 1998. *Critique of Pure Reason.* Translated by P. Guyer and A. Wood. Cambridge: Cambridge University Press.

Jacobi

JWA = Jacobi. Werke. Gesamtausgabe. Edited by Klaus Hammacher and Walter Jaeschke. Hamburg: Meiner, 1998 ff. Cited by volume : page and followed when relevant by translation page number in Jacobi, F. H., 1995. *Main Philosophical Writings and the Novel Allwill* (Vol. 18). McGill-Queen's Press.

Hegel

Brown = Hegel, Lectures on the History of Philosophy 1825–6, vol 3. Edited by Robert F. Brown. Oxford University Press, 2006.

§ or EL = GW 20 / Encyclopedia of the Philosophical Sciences in Basic Outline, Part 1, Science of Logic (Cambridge Hegel Translations). Translated by Klaus Brinkmann and Daniel O. Dahlstrom. Cambridge: Cambridge University Press, 2010. I cite the *Encyclopaedia* by § number, with "An" indicating *Anmerkung* and "Zu" indicating *Zusatz* (from TWA).

GW = Hegel, G. W. F. [GW] 1968 ff. Gesammelte Werke. Edited by The Nordrhein-Westfälische Akademie der Wissenschaften. Hamburg: Meiner (abbreviation GW, indicating first the volume number).

JS = Hegel, Georg Wilhelm Friedrich. 1961. Science of Logic. Translated by W. H. Johnston, and L. G. Struthers. With an Introductory Pref. by Viscount Haldane of Cloane. Allen Unwin.

Mich. = Vorlesungen über die Geschichte der Philosophie. In Werke, vols. 13–15. Edited by C. L Michelet. Berlin: Duncker and Humblot, 1840–1844.

SL = GW 21, 11, and 12 / *Georg Wilhelm Friedrich Hegel: The Science of Logic (Cambridge Hegel Translations)*. Translated by George Di Giovanni. Cambridge: Cambridge University Press, 2010. Cited by GW.

TWA = G. W. F. Hegel. 1970–1. *Werke.* 20 vols. Edited by E. Moldenhauer and K. Michel. Frankfurt: Suhrkamp.

VGP = TWA vols. 18–20 / G. W. F. Hegel. 1995. *Lectures on the History of Philosophy.* Translated by E. S. Haldane and Frances H. Simson. Lincoln: University of Nebraska Press.

VGP25/6 = Vorlesungen über die Geschichte der Philosophie, Teil 4: Philosophie des Mittelalters und der neueren Zeit, hrsg. von P. Garniron Und W. Jaeschke (Ausgewählte Nachschriften und Manuskripte, Bd 9). Hamburg: Meiner, 1986.

References

Bartuschat, W. (2007). Nur Hinein, Nicht Heraus: Hegel über Spinoza. In D. H. Heidemann and C. Krijnen, eds., *Hegel und die Geschichte der Philosophie*. Darmstadt: Wissenschaftliche Buchgesellschaft, pp. 101–15.

Boehm, O. (2014). *Kant's Critique of Spinoza*. Oxford: Oxford University Press.

Caird, J. (1888). *Spinoza*. London: William Blackwood and Sons.

Carnap, R. (1932). Überwindung der Metaphysik durch logische Analyse der Sprache. In Erkenntnis 2, 219–41.

Della Rocca, M. (2008). *Spinoza*. London: Routledge.

Della Rocca, M. (2015). Interpreting Spinoza: The Real Is the Rational. *Journal of the History of Philosophy* 53(3), 523–35.

Della Rocca, M. (2020). *The Parmenidean Ascent*. New York: Oxford University Press.

Earle, W. (1973). The Ontological Argument in Spinoza: Twenty Years Later. In M. Grene, ed., *Spinoza: A Collection of Critical Essays*. Garden City: Anchor Press, pp. 220–26.

Emundts, D. (2018). Die Lehre vom Wesen. Dritter Abschnitt. Die Wirklichkeit. In Quante & Mooren 387–456.

Fleischmann, E. J. (1964). Die Wirklichkeit in Hegels Logik: Ideengechichtliche Beziehungen zu Spinoza. *Zeitschrift für Philosophische Forschung* 18(1), 3–29.

Garrett, D. (1979). Spinoza's "Ontological" Argument. *The Philosophical Review* 88(2), 198–223.

Garrett, D. (2012). A Reply on Spinoza's Behalf. In E. Förster and Y. Melamed, eds., *Spinoza and German Idealism*. Cambridge: Cambridge University Press, pp. 248–64.

Garrett, D. (2018). *Nature and Necessity in Spinoza's Philosophy*. Oxford: Oxford University Press.

Gueroult, M. (1968). *Spinoza: Dieu (Éthique, 1)*. Paris: Aubier-Montaigne.

Harrelson, K. (2009). *The Ontological Argument from Descartes to Hegel*. New York: Humanities Press.

Hegel, G. W. F. (2018). *The Phenomenology of Spirit*, trans. Terry Pinkard. Cambridge: Cambridge University Press.

Henrich, D. (1967). *Der ontologische Gottesbeweis: sein Problem und seine Geschichte in der Neuzeit*. Tübingen: Mohr.

Horstmann, R. P. (1993). Metaphysikkritik bei Hegel und Nietzsche. *Hegel-Studien* 28, 285–301.

Host, A. (2021). The Ontological Argument's Revival in German Idealism (doctoral dissertation), Johns Hopkins University.

Hübner, K. (2015). Spinoza on Negation, Mind-Dependence and the Reality of the Finite. In Y. Melamed, ed., *The Young Spinoza: A Metaphysician in the Making*. Oxford: Oxford University Press, pp. 221–37.

Knappik, F. (2016). Hegel's Essentialism: Natural Kinds and the Metaphysics of Explanation in Hegel's Theory of "the Concept." *European Journal of Philosophy* 24, 760–87.

Koch, A. F. (2018). Das Sein. Erster Abschnitt. Die Qualität. In Quante&Mooren 43–144.

Koch, A. F. (2019). Sein und Existenz. In A. Luckner and S. Ostritsch, eds., *Philosophie der Existenz: Abhandlungen zur Philosophie*. Stuttgart: J.B. Metzler, pp. 47–66.

Koch, A. F. (2022). Hegel's Parmenidean Descent to the Science without Contrary. *Hegel-Studien* 56, 65–95.

Kreines, J. (2004). Hegel's Critique of Pure Mechanism and the Philosophical Appeal of the Logic Project. *European Journal of Philosophy* 12(1), 38–74.

Kreines, J. (2006). Hegel's Metaphysics: Changing the Debate. *Philosophy Compass* 1(5), 466–80.

Kreines, J. (2015). *Reason in the World: Hegel's Metaphysics and Its Philosophical Appeal*. Oxford: Oxford University Press.

Kreines, J. (2020). Hegel: The Reality and Priority of Immanent Teleology. In J. K. McDonough, ed., *Teleology: A History*. Oxford: Oxford University Press, pp. 219–48.

Kreines, J. (2024). Schelling's Critique of Hegel: Options and Responses, in the Spirit of Highlighting Shared Insights. *Society for German Idealism and Romanticism* 7, 26–40.

Kreines, J. (2025a). Reasons for the Importance of the Post-Kantian Idea of a System: Nothing Halfway, Jacobi and Schelling. *International Journal of Philosophical Studies* 32(5), 606–39. doi:10.1080/09672559.2025.2456814.

Kreines, J. (2025b). "The Poison Chalice of Metaphysical Grounding: Jacobi and Hegel as Reversing Contemporary Expectations." *The Hegel Bulletin*. doi:10.1017/hgl.2025.10068 .

Leibniz, G. W. (1989). *Leibniz: Philosophical Essays*. Indianapolis: Hackett.

Lin, M. (2019). *Being and Reason: An Essay on Spinoza's Metaphysics*. New York: Oxford University Press.

Macherey, P. (2011). *Hegel or Spinoza*, trans. Susan Ruddick. Minneapolis: University of Minnesota Press.

McNulty, J. (2022). *Hegel's Logic and Metaphysics*. Cambridge: Cambridge University Press.

Melamed, Y. (2010). Acosmism or Weak Individuals?: Hegel, Spinoza, and the Reality of the Finite. *Journal of the History of Philosophy* 48(1), 77–92.

Melamed, Y. (2012a). *"Omnis determinatio est negatio"* – Determination, Negation and Self-Negation in Spinoza, Kant, and Hegel. In E. Förster and Y. Melamed, eds., *Spinoza and German Idealism*. Cambridge: Cambridge University Press, pp. 175–96.

Melamed, Y. (2012b). Spinoza on Inherence, Causation, and Conception. *Journal of the History of Philosophy* 50(3), 365–86.

Melamed, Y. (2013). The Sirens of Elea: Rationalism, Idealism and Monism in Spinoza. In A. LoLordo and S. Duncan, eds., *The Key Debates of Modern Philosophy*. New York: Routledge, pp. 78–89.

Moyar, D. (2012). Thought and Metaphysics: Hegel's Critical Reception of Spinoza. In E. Förster and Y. Melamed, eds., *Spinoza and German Idealism*. Cambridge: Cambridge University Press, pp. 197–213.

Newlands, S. (2011). Hegel's Idealist Reading of Spinoza. *Philosophy Compass* 6(2), 100–108.

Parkinson, G. H. R. (1977). Hegel, Pantheism, and Spinoza. *Journal of the History of Ideas* 38(3), 449–59.

Primus, K. (2023). Spinoza's Monism II: A Proposal. *Archiv für Geschichte der Philosophie* 105(3), 444–69.

Quante, M. (2018). Die Lehre vom Wesen. Erster Abschnitt. Das Wesen als Reflexion in ihm selbst. In Quante & Mooren 275–324.

Quante, M. and Mooren, N., eds. (2018). *Kommentar zu Hegels Wissenschaft der Logik (Hegel-Studien. Beiheft 67)*. Hamburg: Felix Meiner Verlag.

Rödl, S. (2018). *Self-Consciousness and Objectivity: An Introduction to Absolute Idealism*. Cambridge: Harvard University Press.

Rohs, P. (1972). *Form und Grund: Interpretation eines Kapitels der hegelschen Wissenschaft der Logik*. Hamburg: Felix Meiner Verlag.

Sandkaulen, B. (2000). *Grund und Ursache: Die Vernunftkritik Jacobis*. München: Fink Wilhelm.

Sandkaulen, B. (2008). Die Ontologie der Substanz, der Begriff der Subjektivität und die Faktizität des Einzelnen: Hegels reflexionslogische Widerlegung der Spinozanischen Metaphysik. In K. Ameriks and J. Stolzenberg, eds., *5/2007 Metaphysik / Metaphysics*. Berlin: De Gruyter, pp. 235–75.

Sandkaulen, B. (2019). *Jacobis Philosophie: Über den Widerspruch zwischen System und Freiheit*. Hamburg: Felix Meiner Verlag.

Schaffer, J. (2009), On what grounds what. In D. J. Chalmers, D. Manley, & R. Wasserman (eds.), *Metametaphysics: New Essays on the Foundations of Ontology*. Oxford: Oxford University Press.

Siderits, Mark. (2021). *Buddhism as Philosophy: An Introduction*. Indianapolis: Routledge. 2nd ed., originally 2017.

Siep, L. (2000). *Der Weg der Phänomenologie des Geistes*. Frankfurt: Suhrkamp.

Siep, L. (2018). Die Lehre Vom Begriff. Dritter Abschnitt. In Quante & Mooren (eds.), *Die Idee*. 651-796.

Spinoza, B. (2002). *Spinoza: Complete Works*. Indianapolis: Hackett.

Stein, S. (2021). Absolute Geist or Self-Loving God? In *Hegel's Encyclopedia of the Philosophical Sciences: A Critical Guide*, 270.

Stern, R. (2009). *Hegelian Metaphysics*. Oxford: Oxford University Press.

Van Cleve, J. (1999). *Problems from Kant*. Oxford: Oxford University Press.

Wolfson, H. A. (1934). *The Philosophy of Spinoza: Unfolding the Latent Processes of His Reasoning*. MA: Harvard University Press.

Yovel, Y. (1992). *Spinoza and Other Heretics. Vol. 1*. Princeton: Princeton University Press.

Acknowledgments

Special thanks to Don Garrett, Alex Host, Toni Koch, and Jensen Suther; to audiences at the Freie Universität Berlin, the Humboldt-Universität zu Berlin, the Universität Potsdam, and the University of Toronto; to students and research assistants James Cullers, Emilio Esquivel Marquez, and Abhinav Ganesh; and to members of an online discussion group's generous interlocutors, always arguing.

Cambridge Elements

The Philosophy of Georg Wilhelm Friedrich Hegel

Sebastian Stein
Heidelberg University

Sebastian Stein is a Research Associate at Heidelberg University. He is co-editor of *Hegel's Political Philosophy* (2017), *Hegel and Contemporary Practical Philosophy* (with James Gledhill, 2019) and *Hegel's Encyclopedic System* (2021), and has authored several journal articles and chapters on Aristotle, Kant, post-Kantian idealism and (neo-)naturalism.

Joshua Wretzel
Pennsylvania State University

Joshua Wretzel is Assistant Teaching Professor of Philosophy at the Pennsylvania State University. He is the co-editor of *Hegel's Encyclopedic System* and *Hegel's Encyclopedia of the Philosophical Sciences: A Critical Guide* (Cambridge). His articles on Hegel and the German philosophical tradition have appeared in multiple edited collections and peer-reviewed journals, including the *European Journal of Philosophy* and *International Journal for Philosophical Studies*.

About the Series
These Elements provide insights into all aspects of Hegel's thought and its relationship to philosophical currents before, during, and after his time. They offer fresh perspectives on well-established topics in Hegel studies, and in some cases use Hegelian categories to define new research programs and to complement existing discussions.

Cambridge Elements ≡

The Philosophy of Georg Wilhelm Friedrich Hegel

Elements in the Series

Hegel and Heidegger on Time
Ioannis Trisokkas

Hegel and Colonialism
Daniel James and Franz Knappik

Hegel's Sublation of Transcendental Idealism
Christian Krijnen

Hegel on the Family Form
Andreja Novakovic

Hegel's Philosophy of Nature
Christian Martin

Hegel and Republicanism: Non-Domination, Economics, and Political Participation
Christopher Yeomans

Hegel and Spinoza
James Kreines

A full series listing is available at: www.cambridge.org/EPGH

For EU product safety concerns, contact us at Calle de José Abascal, 56–1°,
28003 Madrid, Spain or eugpsr@cambridge.org.